CONTENTS

Pedigree®

Published by Pedigree Books Limited
Beech Hill House, Walnut Gardens, Exeter, Devon EX4 4DH

POKéMON

DIAMOND AND PEARL

ANNUAL 2009

£7.99

MEET

ASH

Ash Ketchum has promised himself that one day he will become the greatest Pokémon Trainer in the world! Ash was only ten years old when he first left his home in Pallet Town, but he's come a long way since then. He has journeyed through three regions already, learning and perfecting his fighting skills all along the way.

Ash lives for battle. He is competitive and focussed, with a powerful sense of right and wrong. If he sees injustice, Ash will leap in and make a challenge without thinking about the dangers. At times, this recklessness has landed him in trouble, but it has earned him friends too. Ash's belief that Pokémon should be treated with fairness and respect has helped him to build a powerful bond with his Pikachu.

Ash and Pikachu make an unlikely duo, but they are the best of friends! The pair have been battle companions right from the beginning of Ash's training. Although they got off to a shaky start, Ash soon realised that there was something special about this sparky little Electric Pokémon!

Now that Pikachu and Ash have travelled so far together, nothing can split them apart. Pikachu has served his master through many fierce battles, often taking on towering opponents with awesome abilities. Although he is small, this plucky Pokémon has developed his own set of knock-out skills, including Thunderbolt, Iron Tail and Volt Tackle. When Ash decided to make the journey to Sinnoh Region, Pikachu was by his side.

...AND PIKACHU!

MEET

BROCK

Brock is Ash's loyal friend and companion. As well as being an entertaining travel buddy, Brock has an unrivalled knowledge of Pokémon tactics and abilities. This comes from his time as leader of the Pewter City Gym. Brock's battle days are over for now though – his sights are set on becoming an expert Pokémon Breeder! Aside from Pokémon, Brock takes a terrific interest in pretty girls. If a lady approaches the group, Brock is guaranteed to fall head-over-heels in love with her!

DAWN

Ash and Brock met Dawn when they were travelling through Twinleaf Town in the Sinnoh region. Dawn was born in Twinleaf, so it was a big step to join the boys on her first Pokémon journey. The trio are great friends already – when times are tough, Dawn's positive energy and bubbly smile always keeps the group going. After witnessing some battles with her Pokémon Piplup, Dawn has decided to become a Co-ordinator. This means that the Pokémon she enters in competitions will be judged on their beauty rather than their fighting power.

Jessie, James and Meowth are the unsavoury faces behind Team Rocket. The threesome have made it their goal to steal Pikachu and the other Pokémon. They are under orders from their boss Giovanni to steal the yellow Pokémon using whatever dirty tricks they can get away with. Luckily Team Rocket's plans are so half-baked they nearly always go terribly, embarrassingly wrong. Although Jessie insists that they refer to Ash and his pals as the 'Twerps', the name describes their own group much better!

Meowth is a rare Pokémon because it can understand and communicate in human speech. It is Meowth that cooks up most of Team Rocket's ludicrous schemes. James is a poor little rich boy that ran away from his wealthy parents. Jessie is vain, spiteful and obsessed with her looks – definitely the most dangerous member of the bunch.

TEAM ROCKET

SINNOH ISLAND MAP

After his victories in the Battle Frontier, Ash's next adventure takes him to the far-off Sinnoh region. This mountainous land presents him with some of the most formidable enemies and the hardest battle games he has ever encountered. As well as his good friend Brock, Ash selects only Pikachu and Aipom to join him on this perilous new quest!

Ash's latest journey is a white-knuckle ride through new Gyms, Contests and wild terrains. As usual Team Rocket are behind him every step of the way, hoping to seize their chance to snatch Pikachu. As well as old adversaries, Ash also meets a rival Pokémon trainer called Paul. Paul is a force to be reckoned with, but as everyone in Sinnoh is about to discover, this talented Pokémon trainer is going to be even tougher to stop!

1 CYCLING ROAD & WAYWARD CAVE
2 ETERNA CITY
3 ETERNA FOREST
4 FLOARMA TOWN
5 HEARTHOME CITY
6 JUBILIFE CITY
7 MT. CORONET
8 OREBURGH CITY
9 SANDGEM TOWN
10 TWINLEAF TOWN

POKÉDEX CHALLENGE

How well do you know your Pokémon? Look closely at each of these creatures and match them to the correct Pokédex reading.

A. THE DRAGON POKÉMON

As a result of a powerful desire to fly, it was able to trigger the cells in its body to cause it to grow wings.

B. THE EMOTION POKÉMON

It uses the horns on its head to amplify its Psychic Powers and when this occurs reality becomes warped and future events can be seen.

C. THE PENGUIN POKÉMON

It's very proud, and its thick down protects it from the cold.

D. THE AQUARABBIT POKÉMON

It lives in rivers and lakes, and while in water its body's colour and pattern confuses its enemies.

E. THE ELECTRIC POKÉMON

It waves its arms to produce a strong electrical charge, and gains strength when lightning is present.

FIERY DOT-TO-DOT

This page is red hot with Chimchar and its two Pokémon evolutions! Join up the dots up to bring Monferno and Infernape to life. Now look through the book to find the right colours for the trio, or make up your own vivid designs!

001 TURTWIG

TYPE:	GRASS
ABILITY:	OVERGROW
HEIGHT:	0.4m
WEIGHT:	10.2kg

Turtwig's protective shell hardens up whenever it drinks. These earthy Pokémon are often found near water. Turtwig evolves into a Grotle and then a Torterra.

002 GROTLE

TYPE:	GRASS
ABILITY:	OVERGROW
HEIGHT:	1.1m
WEIGHT:	97kg

Grotle's shell is made from hardened soil. In the daytime it comes out to sunbathe, attracting some Pokémon that peck the berries growing on the trees on its back.

003 TORTERRA

TYPE:	GRASS-GROUND
ABILITY:	OVERGROW
HEIGHT:	2.2m
WEIGHT:	310kg

Herds of this Pokémon are sometimes mistaken for moving forests. When Torterra is still, small Pokémon often try and build nests on its back.

004 CHIMCHAR

TYPE:	FIRE
ABILITY:	BLAZE
HEIGHT:	0.5m
WEIGHT:	6.2kg

Chimchar climbs steep cliff faces with natural ease. Its fiery behind is stoked by gas in its belly. This Pokémon's fire is only put out when it settles down to sleep.

005 MONFERNO

TYPE:	FIRE-FIGHTING
ABILITY:	BLAZE
HEIGHT:	0.9m
WEIGHT:	22kg

When confronted, Monferno will stretch the fire in its tail so that it appears more fearsome. It scales ceilings and walls to mount scorching aerial attacks.

006 INFERNAPE

TYPE:	FIRE-FIGHTING
ABILITY:	BLAZE
HEIGHT:	1.2m
WEIGHT:	55kg

The third evolution from Chimchar, Infernape uses all its limbs in a unique form of martial arts. As quick as a flash, this Pokémon truly deserves its crown of fire.

007 PIPLUP

TYPE:	WATER
ABILITY:	TORRENT
HEIGHT:	0.4m
WEIGHT:	5.2kg

Piplup dwells along northern shores, diving for food in the chilly waters. An astonishingly proud creature, it will not allow itself to accept gifts of food.

008 PRINPLUP

TYPE:	WATER
ABILITY:	TORRENT
HEIGHT:	0.8m
WEIGHT:	23kg

A blow from this solitary creature's wings is powerful enough to crack tree trunks. Evolved from Piplup, each one believes that it is the best Pokémon around.

009 EMPOLEON

TYPE:	WATER-STEEL
ABILITY:	TORRENT
HEIGHT:	1.7m
WEIGHT:	84.5kg

Empoleon's three majestic horns indicate the power that it exerts. Empoleon swims faster than a speed boat, with wings sharp enough to pierce floating ice.

010 STARLY

TYPE:	NORMAL-FLYING
ABILITY:	KEEN EYE
HEIGHT:	0.3m
WEIGHT:	2kg

Starly soar in great flocks, but are scarcely noticeable when alone. Each Pokémon has a piercing call and strong wings. Starly evolves into a Staravia and then a Staraptor.

011 STARAVIA

TYPE:	NORMAL-FLYING
ABILITY:	INTIMIDATE
HEIGHT:	0.6m
WEIGHT:	15.5kg

Staravia roams forests and fields, searching out Pokémon bug prey. These territorial birds will start a fierce squabble if another flock strays onto their patch.

012 STARAPTOR

TYPE:	NORMAL-FLYING
ABILITY:	INTIMIDATE
HEIGHT:	1.2m
WEIGHT:	24.9kg

Savage Staraptor has razor-like claws that can easily clench a small Pokémon while it is flying. It seemingly has no fear, often challenging enemies that are twice its size.

013 BIDOOF

TYPE:	NORMAL
ABILITY:	SIMPLE-UNAWARE
HEIGHT:	0.5m
WEIGHT:	20kg

Much more skilful than it first appears, Bidoof spends its time sharpening its teeth on logs and rocks. Nothing phases this brave Pokémon. Bidoof evolves into Bibarel.

014 BIBAREL

TYPE:	NORMAL-WATER
ABILITY:	SIMPLE-UNAWARE
HEIGHT:	1m
WEIGHT:	31.5kg

Bibarel works tirelessly, damming rivers and brooks so it can nest. Out of water it can seem slow and clumsy, but when submerged it swims as fast as any Feebas.

015 KRICKETOT

TYPE:	BUG
ABILITY:	SHED SKIN
HEIGHT:	0.3m
WEIGHT:	2.2kg

This Pokémon communicates by shaking its head, causing its antennae to knock against each other. In Autumn, Sinnoh forests ring with the sound of Kricketot.

016 KRICKETUNE

TYPE:	BUG
ABILITY:	SWARM
HEIGHT:	1m
WEIGHT:	25.5kg

Evolved from Kricketot, Kricketune crosses its knife-like arms when it cries. Scientists' research suggests its bewitching melodies are used to signal its mood.

017 SHINX

TYPE:	ELECTRIC
ABILITY:	RIVALRY-INTIMIDATE
HEIGHT:	0.5m
WEIGHT:	9.5kg

If in danger, Shinx's fur will start to glow and shine. This blinds the foe, giving the Pokémon valuable time to escape. Shinx evolves to a Luxio and then a Luxray.

018 LUXIO

TYPE:	ELECTRIC
ABILITY:	RIVALRY-INTIMIDATE
HEIGHT:	0.9m
WEIGHT:	30.5kg

Its claws emit a series of volts so intense it can cause fainting. Luxio prefers to live in small clans, communicating with electric pulses from its charged forelegs.

019 LUXRAY

TYPE:	ELECTRIC
ABILITY:	RIVALRY-INTIMIDATE
HEIGHT:	1.4m
WEIGHT:	42kg

Luxray's eyes can bore through any substance. When the Pokémon's eyes turn gold and start glowing, it can even spot prey taking shelter behind rocks and walls.

020 ABRA

TYPE:	PSYCHIC
ABILITY:	SYNCHRONISE-INNER FOCUS
HEIGHT:	0.9m
WEIGHT:	19.5kg

Abra sleeps for at least 18 hours a day, never standing up. When it wakes, it only moves via teleportation. Abra evolves into a Kadabra then a Alakazam.

021 KADABRA

TYPE:	PSYCHIC
ABILITY:	SYNCHRONISE-INNER FOCUS
HEIGHT:	1.3m
WEIGHT:	56.5kg

Spotting a Kadabra is said to be a sign of impending bad luck. If this Pokémon is lurking nearby, a strange dark shadow will appear on TV screens in the area.

022 ALAKAZAM

TYPE:	PSYCHIC
ABILITY:	SYNCHRONISE-INNER FOCUS
HEIGHT:	1.5m
WEIGHT:	48kg

This creature has an enormous intellect, boasting an IQ in excess of 5,000. Its brilliant mind allows it to remember everything it has experienced from birth.

023 MAGIKARP

TYPE:	WATER
ABILITY:	SWIFT SWIM
HEIGHT:	0.9m
WEIGHT:	10kg

Nobody can understand why the vulnerable Magikarp was not made extinct centuries ago. It is possibly the weakest Pokémon in the world.

024 GYARADOS

TYPE:	WATER-FLYING
ABILITY:	INTIMIDATE
HEIGHT:	6.5m
WEIGHT:	235kg

Evolved from Magikarp, Gyarados is a creature of dread. Prone to terrible rages, it won't rest until it has destroyed anything and everything in its way.

025 BUDEW

TYPE:	GRASS-POISON
ABILITY:	NATURAL CURE-POISON POINT
HEIGHT:	0.2m
WEIGHT:	1.2kg

Those that breathe in Budew's pollen can suffer from sneezing fits and runny noses. Budew hibernates in winter, closing its bud to shelter from the freezing weather.

026 ROSELIA

TYPE:	GRASS-POISON
ABILITY:	NATURAL CURE-POISON POINT
HEIGHT:	0.3m
WEIGHT:	2kg

Roselia is evolved from a Budew, transforming again into a Roserade. It needs a good supply of clean water for its vibrantly-coloured blooms to flower.

027 ROSERADE

TYPE:	GRASS-POISON
ABILITY:	NATURAL CURE-POISON POINT
HEIGHT:	0.9m
WEIGHT:	14.5kg

Roserade's prey can't resist its heady scent. The swaying Pokémon hides its thorny whips behind it, then strikes poison barbs when its victim least expects it.

028 ZUBAT

TYPE:	POISON-FLYING
ABILITY:	INNER FOCUS
HEIGHT:	0.8m
WEIGHT:	7.5kg

This blind Pokémon uses ultrasonic pulses to make up for its lack of sight. It senses obstacles via waves emitted from its jaw. It evolves into a Golbat and then a Crobat.

029 GOLBAT

TYPE:	POISON-FLYING
ABILITY:	INNER FOCUS
HEIGHT:	1.6m
WEIGHT:	55kg

Golbat prowls the skies each and every night, searching for juicy neck veins. The fierce-fanged creature craves the blood of both humans and Pokémon.

030 CROBAT

TYPE:	POSION-FLYING
ABILITY:	INNER FOCUS
HEIGHT:	1.8m
WEIGHT:	75kg

This bat-like creature has four sleek wings, enabling it to glide silently and at terrific speeds. Crobat rests during the day, becoming active again at sunset.

031 GEODUDE

TYPE:	ROCK-GROUND
ABILITY:	ROCK HEAD-STURDY
HEIGHT:	0.4m
WEIGHT:	20kg

Most Geodude live on rocky mountain passes, half-buried in the rubble. Geodude covers itself in stones so that it can spy on approaching climbers.

032 GRAVELER

TYPE:	ROCK-GROUND
ABILITY:	ROCK HEAD-STURDY
HEIGHT:	1m
WEIGHT:	105kg

Graveler uses its powerful grey arms to channel out rough holes in cliff faces. Once it has tunnelled into the rock, it will clamber in and set up home.

033 GOLEM

TYPE:	ROCK-GROUND
ABILITY:	ROCK HEAD-STURDY
HEIGHT:	1.4m
WEIGHT:	300kg

Golem sheds its thick hide once a year. Even dynamite cannot blast a dent in its boulder-like body. It is evolved from a Geodude and then a Graveler.

034 ONIX

TYPE:	ROCK-GROUND
ABILITY:	ROCK HEAD-STURDY
HEIGHT:	8.8m
WEIGHT:	210kg

A powerful snake-like Pokémon, Onix can tunnel at over 80 km/h. It travels with such force, the ground rumbles and shakes with the aftershock. Onix evolves into a Steelix.

035 STEELIX

TYPE:	STEEL-GROUND
ABILITY:	ROCK HEAD-STURDY
HEIGHT:	9.2m
WEIGHT:	400kg

The high pressure and intense heat of burrowing deep underground has had a profound effect on Steelix. Its body is harder than any known metal.

036 CRANIDOS

TYPE:	ROCK
ABILITY:	MOULD BREAKER
HEIGHT:	0.9m
WEIGHT:	31.5kg

Cranidos roamed the jungles around 100 million years ago, but was resurrected from an iron ball-like fossil. The Pokémon uses its iron-hard head to butt victims.

037 RAMPARDOS

TYPE:	ROCK
ABILITY:	MOULD BREAKER
HEIGHT:	1.6m
WEIGHT:	102.5kg

Evolved from Cranidos, Rampardos has a head butt so forceful it can shatter most objects. It is a violent brute that will rip out trees as it rampages through the jungle.

038 SHIELDON

TYPE:	ROCK-STEEL
ABILITY:	STURDY
HEIGHT:	0.5m
WEIGHT:	57kg

Shieldon is a prehistoric beast with a tough plated face. It polishes its face by rubbing it up and down jungle tree trunks. Shieldon is weak when ambushed from behind.

039 BASTIODON

TYPE:	ROCK-STEEL
ABILITY:	STURDY
HEIGHT:	1.3m
WEIGHT:	149.5kg

Bastiodon is a large but docile Pokémon that spends its time grazing for grass and berries. If attacked, it will use its hard, block-shaped face to shield its young.

040 MACHOP

TYPE:	FIGHTING
ABILITY:	GUTS-NO GUARD
HEIGHT:	0.8m
WEIGHT:	19.5kg

Machop is expertly skilled in every form of martial arts. To build up strength, it weightlifts using a Graveler. Machop evolves into a Machoke and then a Machamp.

CRAZY COLOUR COPY

Which Pokémon have joined Ash in this colour copy grid? Copy the pictures into the large box in the correct alphabetical order to find out!

18

STOP
TEAM ROCKET!

Jessie, James and Meowth are trying to get their hands on Pikachu again! Help the Pokémon get back to his friends by tracing the words that describe Team Rocket's wicked ways.

SLY
FRIENDLY
LOYAL
WELCOMING
CALM
ENJOYABLE
DEVIOUS
PATIENT
NICE
CHEATING
PEACEFUL
CHEERFUL
SKILFUL
SCHEMING
CONSIDERATE
LAZY
JEALOUS
TRUSTWORTHY
WARM
CARING
MEAN
HAPPY
DISLOYAL
AMUSING
KIND
GENTLE
SELFISH
TALENTED
PLEASING
GENEROUS
THOUGHTFUL
CHEERFUL
THOUGHTLESS
PEACEFUL
SMILEY
JOYFUL
GENTLE
SOCIABLE
HARSH
BIG-HEARTED
AGREEABLE
DISHONEST

SHAPES
OF THINGS TO COME!

OUR HEROES HAVE TREKKED FOR DAYS SO THAT ASH CAN TAKE ON HIS FIRST SINNOH BATTLE, BUT WHAT KIND OF COMPETITORS WILL THEY FIND WAITING FOR THEM IN THE OREBURGH GYM?

Ash, Brock and Dawn stared down at the valley in front of them. "There it is guys," cried Ash. "Oreburgh City!" "Sure looks like a great place to have your first Sinnoh battle," said Dawn. "Also a great place to get my first badge!" Ash grinned, then turned back to Pikachu. "Whaddaya say?" Pikachu chirruped excitedly at his master.

The friends headed straight for the Gym. It was pretty impressive. Dawn frowned. "Doesn't look like the kind of gym you'd challenge unless you were serious about it!" "Yeah?" psyched Ash. "Well then that's for me!" Suddenly the gym doors opened… and Paul came towards them! Everyone gasped as a man behind him asked, "Are these friends of yours?" "No way!" muttered Paul. Ash stepped forward. "I've come from Pallet Town. It's great to be here!" "Welcome to Oreburgh Gym, " the man smiled. "The temple for Rock Pokémon."

The man led them inside. "My name is Ian and I take care of the Pokémon around here." "So that means you can't be the Gym Leader?" cried Ash. Paul looked at Ash as if he was an imbecile. "Duh!" "You've got it!" laughed Ian. "Our Leader's name is Roark, but he's not here right now." As Paul stomped off to the Pokémon Centre, Ian led the gang inside. He presented Ash with a small metal box. "Here's your Sinnoh region badge case," he explained. "If

you win eight badges, you can compete in the Sinnoh League." "Thanks!" beamed Ash, before his curiosity got the better of him. "Hey Ian, do ya mind if I ask where Roark is?" "He's coal mining!" explained Ian. Ash looked blank. "Makes sense to me!" cried Brock. "I've heard Oreburgh City has some of the richest coal anywhere." Ian nodded. "And while Roark digs for coal, he's exploring for hidden treasure."

Hidden Treasure? Ash and his friends decided to check the Oreburgh mine out for themselves. Unfortunately Team Rocket had got there first.

"Listen!" called Jessie. "Is that big money calling from below?"

James smirked. "The sound of success tells me so!"

Jessie smoothed down her overalls and lifted her spade. "Sock it away at a breakneck pace."

"Putting big bucks in poverty's place!" chipped in James.

Jessie, James and Meowth crossed shovels in the air. "We're Team Rocket and we're on a roll!"

Jessie sunk her spade into the ground and made a terrible discovery. Mining was hard labour!

She stamped her feet in a furious tantrum. "This work hard, another day another dollar stuff may work for you, but for me it *stinks!*"

"Excuse me," said Ash. "We heard that Roark was here. Is that true?"

Team Rocket were not impressed.

"It's the erp-Tway and all of his little end-frays!" sneered James.

A team of workers wheeled a mining car past, loaded with iron ore. At the far end of the tracks, a foreman in a red helmet signalled for them to stop.

"OK Roark," shouted one of the miners.

Roark! Ash's eyes widened – what was the Gym Leader doing here?

Roark was not ready to explain himself just yet. Instead he was gazing in awe at a fossil etched into one of the coal boulders. "Welcome, from your century to mine," he whispered. "One day I know you'll come back to life."

Team Rocket stopped in their tracks. "Did he say back to life?"

A passing miner overheard them. "Oh yes, there's an incredible machine that resurrects ancient Pokémon fossils!"

Jessie dragged her crew behind a rock. " We gotta steal that machine!"

Roark waved to Ash and his friends. "That fossil is treasure. That's why I enjoy my work as a foreman here."

Back at the Oreburgh Gym, Ian was waiting for Roark and his new friends. "Welcome back," he smiled. "How was the treasure hunt?"

Roark's face lit up. "We really discovered something this time. Maybe the best fossil yet!"

Ian pointed to the doorway. "Here's your first challenger."

Paul stepped forward, but as soon as he spotted Ash he scowled and turned away.

"I'm sorry to keep you waiting," said Roark. "Why don't we get started."

"I can't wait to see a Gym Battle!" shrieked Dawn. Ash, Pikachu and Brock were speechless.

"You've never seen one?" asked Roark.

"No," cried Dawn, "but I want to learn everything about them that I can!"

"Well it's fine with me," agreed the Gym Leader. "Hey Paul, how about you?"

Paul didn't even stop to look back. "I really couldn't care less."

Ash was fired up now. "You can be sure I'll be watching you guys battle!"

GEODUDE
THE ROCK POKÉMON

GEODUDE IS OFTEN FOUND ON MOUNTAIN ROADS WITH HALF OF ITS BODY BURIED IN THE GROUND, SO IT CAN OBSERVE MOUNTAIN TRAVELLERS.

Sunshine burst through as the ceiling parted over the Oreburgh Gym. "Awesome," exclaimed Dawn. "So this is what it's like in a gym!" "When it comes to battlefields there are all sorts of types," explained Brock. "This is a Rock-type gym." Roark and Paul took their places at each end of the battlefield. Ian raised his arms. "The Oreburgh City Gym battle between Paul the challenger and Roark the Gym Leader is about to get underway!" he announced. "The battle will be three on three, as soon as all three Pokémon on either side are unable to continue the challenge is over! Only the challenger may substitute Pokémon." Ash held his breath as everyone waited for Ian's signal. "Now let the battle begin!" Roark was up first, hurling his Poké Ball into the centre. "Oh wow," cried Dawn. "It's a Geodude!" She looked it up in her Pokédex.

AZUMARILL
THE AQUARABBIT
POKÉMON

AZUMARILL LIVES IN RIVERS AND LAKES, AND WHILE IN WATER ITS BODY COLOUR AND PATTERN CONFUSES ITS ENEMIES.

Paul didn't flinch. "Azumarill, stand by!"
"So Paul's using a water-type Pokémon," whispered Ash.
Dawn showed him her Pokédex.

"Since Water-type moves are really powerful against Rock-type Pokémon, Azumarill's a smart choice," said Brock, admiringly.
"Then Paul's got the upper hand, right?" asked Dawn.
Brock chuckled. "In theory."
"Paul, You have the honour," invited Roark generously.
The challenger accepted the first move.
"Azumarill, Hydro Pump. Go!"
"Geodude," ordered Roark. "Hidden Power!"
Azumarill pounded its enemy with a drilling tower of water. Torrents of gushing liquid came shooting out of its mouth in a relentless jet. The Rock Pokémon shielded its head then clenched its fists in retaliation. Suddenly Geodude released its Hidden Power move, showering Azumarill with a barrage of crystallised rocks.

Everyone was blinded by the shattering white light streaming from Geodude's mighty fists. The rock blows sent Azurmarill reeling to the ground. Ash gasped. "It beat back that Hydro Pump!"

"And that was a Water-type move too," added Brock.
Roark was straight into his next move. "All right Geodude, Rollout!"
"Water Gun Azumarill!' urged Paul

Geodude curled up like a balling ball, skittling Azumarill before it could make its next move." Brock nodded appreciatively. "Not giving his challengers any time for counter attacks is how Roark keeps up the pressure!" Geodude rammed its foe again, sending the Pokémon high into the air. Ian stood up. "Azumarill is unable to battle! Geodude wins!"
Dawn was totally confused. "A Water-type Pokémon just lost to a Rock-type?"
"Unbelievable," mused Brock, "to get a knock-out on the second attack!"
"Now I understand what you meant before when you said that Paul had an upper hand in theory," said Dawn.

Paul furiously summoned Azumarill back to its Poké Ball. "You good for nothing…" "Creep!" muttered Ash. He didn't like the way this kid was talking. In seconds the ball was spinning back onto the battlefield. "Elekid, stand by!"

Roark paused. "I'm sure Paul knows that Elekid's Electric-type moves won't work very well on Geodude. I wonder what he's got up his sleeve?" Paul skilfully selected a Fighting-type move. "Elekid Brick Break!"

"Clever!" yelled Roark. "But we're still going to stick with using Rollout!" Volts crackled around Elekid as it delivered a power blow to its opponent. Geodude was instantly knocked out by the force of the attack. "Geodude is unable to battle!" shouted Ian. "Elekid wins!" Dawn turned to Brock. "I thought Elekid was at a huge disadvantage?" "That goes to show that you can overcome just about any disadvantage with the right moves," replied Brock. Roark gently called in his Pokémon. "Thanks a lot, good friend."

"Onix, you're up next!" ordered Roark.
A giant stone worm snaked up to the sky.
"It's huge!" cried Dawn, flicking open her Pokédex.

ONIX
THE ROCK SNAKE POKÉMON

IT TUNNELS THROUGH THE GROUND, WHICH SHAKES WHEN IT RAISES ITS THUNDEROUS ROAR. IT CAN MOVE THROUGH THE GROUND AT 80 KILOMETRES PER HOUR.

"This Onix can do it," decided Brock. "I raised one myself and I can tell this Pokémon has been through some very tough battles." If he was worried, Paul didn't show it. "I'll be keeping my Elekid." Elekid launched into a new Brick Break, but Onix dodged out of its reach. "How can something so big move so quickly?" marvelled Dawn. "Now use Slam Onix!" bellowed Roark. "Protect!" hissed Paul. Elekid instantly folded its arms across its chest and covered itself in an impenetrable forcefield. Even the weight of Onix couldn't break through. Roark was quick with his counter-move. "Double-edge, let's go!" Onix caught its foe just as its protective barrier went down, but the force of the Double-edge had weakened it. Paul barked at Elekid. "Stay strong, or else!"

back and choose another Pokémon, that one will take all the damage."
"Right!" buzzed Brock. "Looks like Roark is taking care of Paul's substitutions before they happen."
Onix moved in with a Slam, then suddenly froze in a fizz of sparks. When it touched Elekid, it had been paralysed!
"It's called Static," said Brock. "A special ability of Elekid's."
Roark wasn't giving in. "Sometimes moves can be used even when paralysed." Both Pokémon locked again in combat, but this time Onix was the victor. Elekid stumbled onto its knees, drained of power.
"Elekid is a resilient Pokémon," praised Roark.

Roark was keeping up the pressure. "Stealth Rock, Go!"
"Elekid, look out!" warned Ash.
Razor-sharp barbs of light darted around Paul's Pokémon, but it seemed unharmed. Ash and Dawn both turned to Brock.
"Stealth Rock causes damage to Pokémon that appear later in battle," he explained.
Dawn gasped. "You mean if Paul decides to call Elekid

Paul angrily summoned Elekid. "What's Paul doing?" stuttered Dawn. Brock shrugged. "I guess he doesn't care about the Stealth Rock."
"He doesn't care if his next Pokémon gets hurt or not!" cut in Ash. Paul flung his Poké Ball into the field. "Chimchar, stand by!"
"A Fire-Type next eh?" quizzed Roark. "Impressive the way that you come at me with Pokémon that aren't considered very good match-ups."
"Chimchar use Dig!" yelled Paul.
The Pokémon tunnelled into the ground, disorientating Onix.
"Try to sense where Chimchar is moving!" instructed Roark.

Roark looked uneasy. "When will this Static wear off?" As Onix scoured the ground, Paul moved in for the final strike.
"Chimchar, do it!" Suddenly, Chimchar burst from the ground, throwing Onix backwards. It was a knock-out.

"Onix is unable to battle!" declared Ian. "Chimchar wins." Roark smiled graciously, then summoned Onix. "You were great. Take a nice long rest!" Paul was giving the Gym Leader a run for his money!

It was time for Roark to bring out his final Pokémon.
"Cranidos, let's go!"
Ash reached for his Pokédex. "Cranidos looks just like that fossil we saw."
"Roark, I can read you like a book," muttered Paul slyly.
"Chimchar use Dig!"
"Cranidos, Headbutt now!" thundered Roark.
Chimchar tunnelled furiously through the earth, but Cranidos was ready for it. The stocky grey Pokémon released a terrible blow that sent Chimchar spinning back to Paul's feet.
Brock leapt up. "Cranidos is anticipating Chimchar's movements!"
Paul sent Chimchar to dig again, but this time Cranidos responded with a super-powerful Zen Headbutt.

CRANIDOS
THE HEAD BUTT POKÉMON

CRANIDOS LIVED DEEP IN THE WOODS ABOUT ONE HUNDRED MILLION YEARS AGO, AND ITS CRANIUM IS AS HARD AS STEEL!

Its skull glowed blue as it knocked the Fire Pokémon back to the floor.
"Quick Chimchar, use dig!" barked Paul.
But Chimchar didn't respond. It sat trembling, rooted to the spot.

"Chimchar's so scared, it can't hear anything that Paul is saying," said Brock. "Focus Energy," commanded Roark. Brock grimaced. "I think Roark's planning to use one shot to knock out his opponent!" "You gotta get Chimchar out of there!" shouted Ash. Suddenly Chimchar covered itself in a blanket of flame. "I was waiting for this!" grinned Paul. "Blaze is a special ability that makes Chimchar's Fire-type moves much stronger when its endurance is low!" chipped in Brock. Chimchar hurtled towards Cranidos.

"Now Flame Wheel!" instructed Paul. "Aim for the legs!" Cranidos was catapulted into the dust. Ash gasped. "That Flame Wheel's strong." The battle was fast and furious. Both Pokémon were sent back into attack with move after move. A headbutt from Cranidos delivered the final blow. "Dodge it quick!" cried Paul. It was too late for Chimchar. "Cranidos wins!" announced Ian. Paul looked at his Pokémon in disgust. "Chimchar! I'll deal with you later."

Paul used all his strength to throw his Poké Ball back into the ring.
"Elekid, stand by!"
The Pokémon sprung into the battlefield. Onix's rocks suddenly rose up out of nowhere and pummelled him to the ground.
Dawn squealed in shock.
"Was that Stealth Rock?"
"Yup!" replied Brock.
"Once you use it, the effects just keep going."

"Brick Break!" urged Paul. Roark tried to come back at Paul with Flame Thrower, but Elekid had already hit Cranidos' leg. Cranidos looked defeated, but somehow he found the strength to throw himself into the fight again.
"You've just witnessed Cranidos' special ability, Mould Breaker, ruining *your* special ability!" yelled Roark. Paul and Roark's Pokémon continued in their bitter

combat, until Cranidos began to show signs of weakness.
"Cranidos' attack power seems to be totally dependent on the strength of its legs," whispered Dawn.
"Brick Break again!" commanded Paul.
"Cranidos!" called Roark.
"Flamethrower!"
Wind rushed through the Oreburgh gym as the Pokémon spun and struggled in an intense fight.

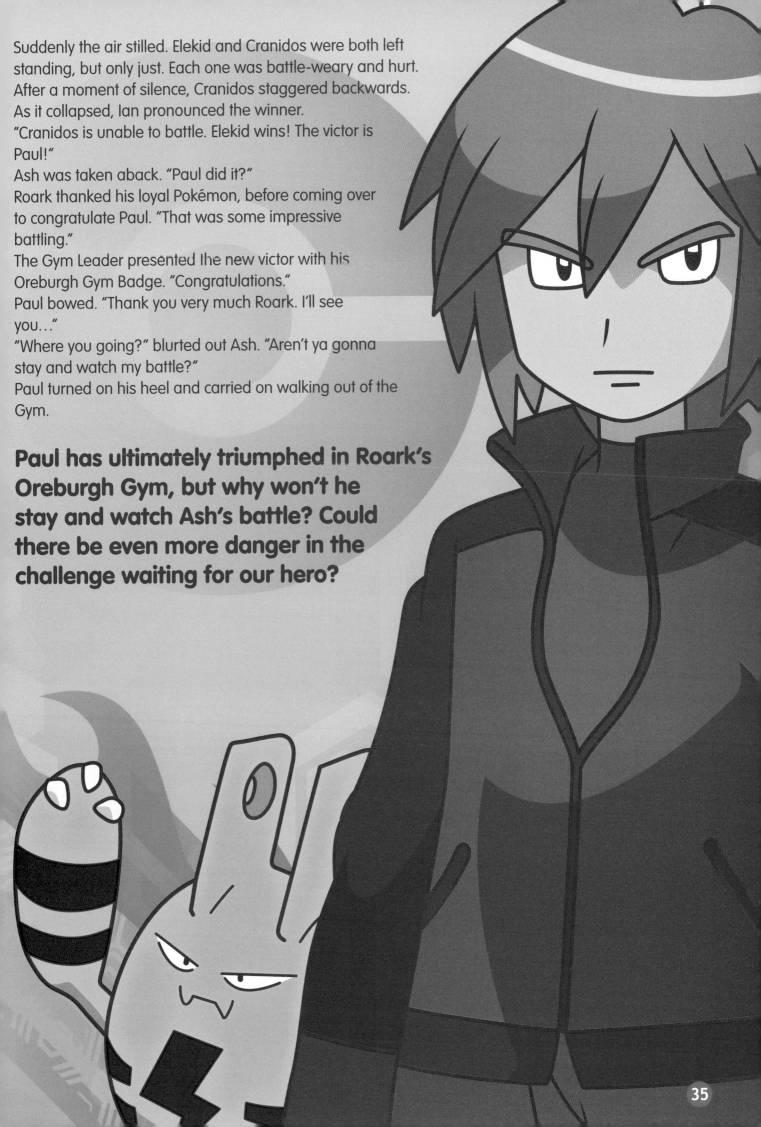

Suddenly the air stilled. Elekid and Cranidos were both left standing, but only just. Each one was battle-weary and hurt. After a moment of silence, Cranidos staggered backwards. As it collapsed, Ian pronounced the winner.

"Cranidos is unable to battle. Elekid wins! The victor is Paul!"

Ash was taken aback. "Paul did it?"

Roark thanked his loyal Pokémon, before coming over to congratulate Paul. "That was some impressive battling."

The Gym Leader presented Ihe new victor with his Oreburgh Gym Badge. "Congratulations."

Paul bowed. "Thank you very much Roark. I'll see you…"

"Where you going?" blurted out Ash. "Aren't ya gonna stay and watch my battle?"

Paul turned on his heel and carried on walking out of the Gym.

Paul has ultimately triumphed in Roark's Oreburgh Gym, but why won't he stay and watch Ash's battle? Could there be even more danger in the challenge waiting for our hero?

35

ROCK-HARD ANAGRAMS

CAN YOU IDENTIFY EACH OF THESE ROCK POKÉMON? STUDY THEIR SHADOWS, THEN UNSCRAMBLE THE LETTERS UNDERNEATH. THEN CIRCLE THE THREE POKÉMON THAT ROARK USED IN HIS BATTLE AT THE OREBURGH CITY GYM!

VELRARGE
⬡⬡⬡⬡⬡⬡⬡⬡

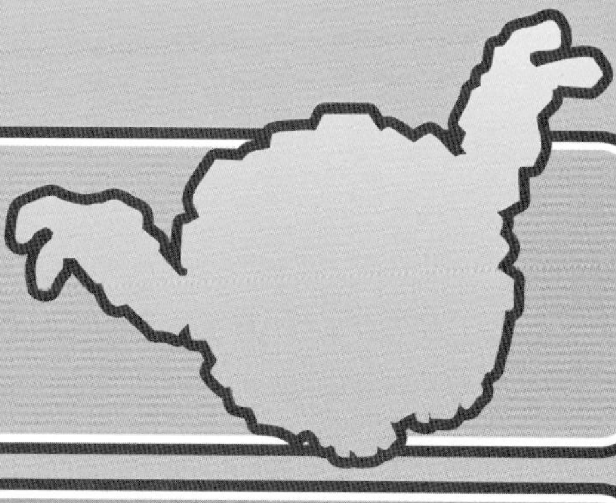

SOBLYN
⬡⬡⬡⬡⬡⬡

TADBONOIS
⬡⬡⬡⬡⬡⬡⬡⬡⬡

ARDSONIC
⬡⬡⬡⬡⬡⬡⬡⬡

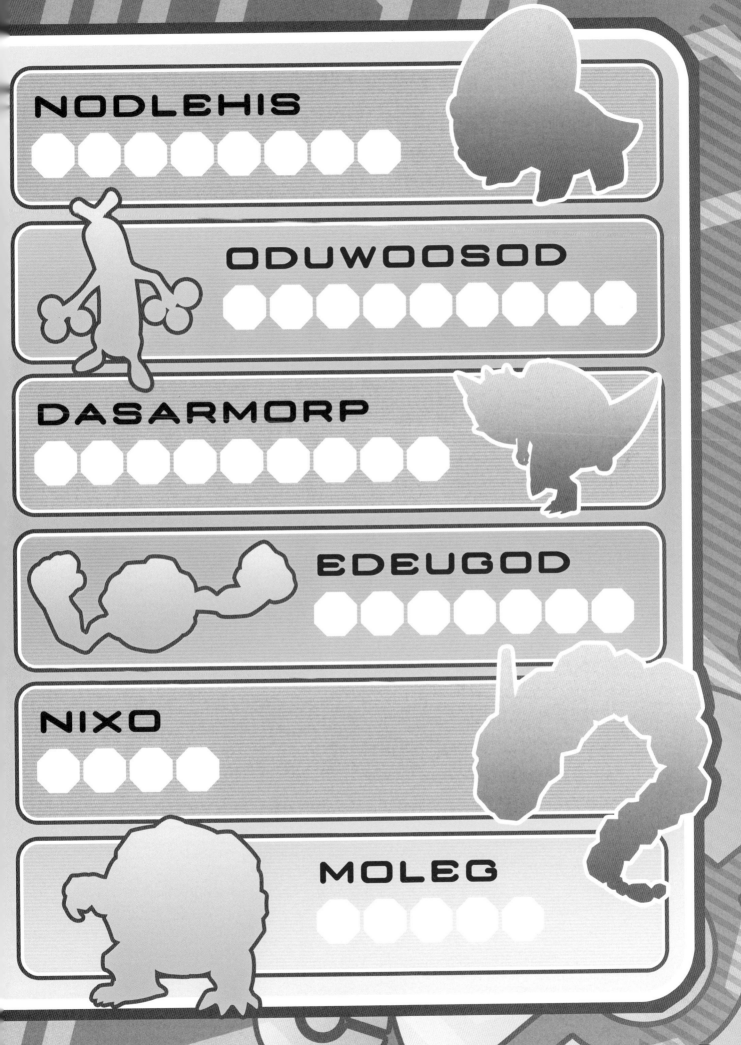

NODLEHIS

ODUWOOSOD

DASARMORP

EDEUGOD

NIXO

MOLEG

041 MACHOKE

TYPE:	FIGHTING
ABILITY:	GUTS-NO GUARD
HEIGHT:	1.5m
WEIGHT:	70.5kg

Machoke is pumped with so much boundless power, it is potentially dangerous. To keep its excessive energy under control, it wears a restraining belt.

042 MACHAMP

TYPE:	FIGHTING
ABILITY:	GUTS-NO GUARD
HEIGHT:	1.6m
WEIGHT:	130kg

Machamp is equipped with four muscled arms that it can wield at lightning speed. This Pokémon can pummel its prey with 1,000 punches in just two seconds.

043 PSYDUCK

TYPE:	WATER
ABILITY:	DAMP-CLOUD NINE
HEIGHT:	0.8m
WEIGHT:	19.6kg

Psyduck is regularly plagued by headaches and bouts of forgetfulness. If the pain gets too intense for it, the Pokémon starts behaving oddly and exhibiting strange powers.

044 GOLDUCK

TYPE:	WATER
ABILITY:	DAMP-CLOUD NINE
HEIGHT:	1.7m
WEIGHT:	76.6kg

Golduck is invariably found in lakes. Evolved from the curious Psyduck, it has the ability to plough through the water faster than any human swimming champion.

045 BURMY

PLANT CLOAK SAND CLOAK TRASH CLOAK

TYPE:	BUG
ABILITY:	SHED SKIN
HEIGHT:	0.2m
WEIGHT:	3.4kg

Burmy covers itself in a thick cloak of leaves and twigs so it can withstand bitter winter gales. The three types it can form are Plant Cloak, Sandy Cloak and Trash Cloak.

046 WORMADAM

SAND CLOAK
PLANT CLOAK TRASH CLOAK

TYPE:	BUG-GRASSS, BUG-STEEL, BUG-FLYING
ABILITY:	ANTICIPATION
HEIGHT:	0.5m
WEIGHT:	6.5kg

When Burmy evolved, its cloak becomes a permanent part of Wormadam's body. Its cloak varies dependent on where it evolved , and what materials are on hand.

047 MOTHIM

TYPE:	BUG-FLYING
ABILITY:	SWARM
HEIGHT:	0.9m
WEIGHT:	23.3kg

Constantly on the move, Mothim is on a perpetual quest to find honey. It flits over field and forest, searching for fertile flowers. It often will steal honey from Combee.

048 WURMPLE

TYPE:	BUG
ABILITY:	SHIELD DUST
HEIGHT:	0.3m
WEIGHT:	3.6kg

Wurmple loves to munch on green leaves. Occasionally Starly will make an attempt to attack it, but the Pokémon's spiked behind is an efficient defensive weapon.

049 SILCOON

TYPE:	BUG
ABILITY:	SHED SKIN
HEIGHT:	0.6m
WEIGHT:	10kg

One of Wurmple's two descendants, Silcoon uses its body silk to bind itself to tree branches. It will then hang motionless, waiting the next stage in its evolution.

050 BEAUTIFLY

TYPE:	BUG-FLYING
ABILITY:	SWARM
HEIGHT:	1m
WEIGHT:	28.4kg

Beautifly uses its thin curled mouth to stab its prey. After a single jab it is able to drain the victim's body fluids, before moving on to its next attack.

051 CASCOON

TYPE:	BUG
ABILITY:	SHED SKIN
HEIGHT:	0.7m
WEIGHT:	11.5kg

Evolved from Wurmple alongside Silcoon, this Pokémon bug uses every cell in its body in the evolution process. It is intensely hot inside its tight silk cocoon.

052 DUSTOX

TYPE:	BUG-POISON
ABILITY:	SHIELD DUST
HEIGHT:	1.2m
WEIGHT:	31.6kg

Dustox is a nocturnal creature. It is often spotted flitting through urban towns and cities, mesmerised by the streetlights. It feeds on leaves and shrubs.

053 COMBEE

TYPE:	BUG-FLYING
ABILITY:	HONEY GATHER
HEIGHT:	0.3m
WEIGHT:	5.5kg

Combee is uniquely formed from three other Pokémon. It buzzes tirelessly from flower to flower, collecting drops of sweet honey to present to Vespiquen.

054 VESPIQUEN

TYPE:	BUG-FLYING
ABILITY:	PRESSURE
HEIGHT:	1.2m
WEIGHT:	38.5kg

Vespiquen's abdomen is a moving six-cell honeycomb for grubs. If threatened the grubs will join the counter-attack. There is only one Vespiquen in each bug colony.

055 PACHIRISU

TYPE:	ELECTRIC
ABILITY:	RUN AWAY-PICKUP
HEIGHT:	0.4m
WEIGHT:	3.9kg

Pachirisu generates electricity in its cheek pouches. This tree-dwelling Pokémon can shoot charges from its bushy tail. It makes fur balls that crackle with static electricity.

056 BUIZEL

TYPE:	WATER
ABILITY:	SWIFT SWIM
HEIGHT:	0.7m
WEIGHT:	29.5kg

Buizel's collar is an effective flotation sac, allowing it to drift on top of water. It rotates its two tails to swim, but will deflate the flotation sac when diving for food.

057 FLOATZEL

TYPE:	WATER
ABILITY:	SWIFT SWIM
HEIGHT:	1.1m
WEIGHT:	33.5kg

It evolved its flotation sac from Buizel so effectively, the sac can double as a life raft. When it is not pursing aquatic prey, Floatzel will dive in to rescue drowning people.

058 CHERUBI

TYPE:	GRASS
ABILITY:	CHLOROPHYLL
HEIGHT:	0.4m
WEIGHT:	3.3kg

Cherubi is coloured red by sunlight. When all the nutrients are drained from its ball, Cherubi shrivels in readiness for evolution.

059 CHERRIM

TYPE:	GRASS
ABILITY:	FLOWER GIFT
HEIGHT:	0.5m
WEIGHT:	9.3kg

When it blooms, Cherrim is a cheerful Pokémon that thrives in bright sunshine. As shadows fall across it, Cherrim will cover its face and fold back into a bud.

060 SHELLOS

TYPE:	WATER
ABILITY:	STICKY HOLD-STORM DRAIN
HEIGHT:	0.3m
WEIGHT:	6.3kg

EAST SEA   WEST SEA

Shellos varies in colour and shape from region to region. Both a blue and a pink form of the Pokémon have been sighted in Sinnoh. Shellos always lives alongside water.

061 GASTRODON

EAST SEA   WEST SEA

TYPE:	WATER-GROUND
ABILITY:	STICKY HOLD-STORM DRAIN
HEIGHT:	0.9m
WEIGHT:	29.9kg

Descended from Shellos, Gastrodon hasn't got a single bone in its body. If any part of the Pokémon is torn off in battle, it regrows again. It lives in shallow rock pools.

062 HERACROSS

TYPE:	BUG-FIGHTING
ABILITY:	SWARM-GUTS
HEIGHT:	1.5m
WEIGHT:	54kg

Heracross thirsts for tree sap. Colonies of the bugs will gather in forests to search out sap to drink. Heracross's powerful horn can easily hurl enemies through the air.

063 AIPOM

TYPE:	NORMAL
ABILITY:	RUN AWAY-PICKUP
HEIGHT:	0.8m
WEIGHT:	11.5kg

Aipom relies on its tail more than its hands. The super-developed extra limb is perfect for plucking fruit out of high trees. Aipom evolves into an Ambipom.

064 AMBIPOM

TYPE:	NORMAL
ABILITY:	TECHNICIAN-PICKUP
HEIGHT:	1.2m
WEIGHT:	20.3kg

This Pokémon has grown a pair of powerful tails to help it eat, travel and fight. At feeding time, its tails are able to pick and shell a pile of nuts within seconds.

065 DRIFLOON

TYPE:	GHOST-FLYING
ABILITY:	AFTERMATH-UNBURDEN
HEIGHT:	0.4m
WEIGHT:	1.2kg

Drifloon is most comfortable in damp, humid climates. It is formed from the spirits of humans and Pokémon. Its attempts to steal children away nearly always backfire.

066 DRIFBLIM

TYPE:	GHOST-FLYING
ABILITY:	AFTERMATH-UNBURDEN
HEIGHT:	1.2m
WEIGHT:	15kg

Drowsy by day-time, at dusk flocks of Drifblim start to drift across the skies. It will carry people and Pokémon, but each aimless journey can end up anywhere.

067 BUNEARY

TYPE:	NORMAL
ABILITY:	RUN AWAY-KLUTZ
HEIGHT:	0.4m
WEIGHT:	5.5kg

Buneary rolls its ears up and then sharply releases them to lash out at its enemies. On cold evenings, the Pokémon sleeps with its head tucked into its furry white body.

068 LOPUNNY

TYPE:	NORMAL
ABILITY:	CUTE CHARM-KLUTZ
HEIGHT:	1.2m
WEIGHT:	33.3kg

This extremely nervous Pokémon will hide underneath its fluffy ear fur it is frightened. Evolved from Buneary, Lopunny is meticulous about grooming.

069 GASTLY

TYPE:	GHOST-POISON
ABILITY:	LEVITATE
HEIGHT:	1.3m
WEIGHT:	0.1kg

Ninety-five per cent of Gastly's body is composed of gases. In a strong gust of wind, it can be totally blown away. Gastly evolves into a Haunter and then a Gengar.

070 HAUNTER

TYPE:	GHOST-POISON
ABILITY:	LEVITATE
HEIGHT:	1.6m
WEIGHT:	0.1kg

Haunter's vaporous body can pass through any obstacle that blocks its path. This Pokémon spies on its enemies by hiding unnoticed inside walls or behind trees.

071 GENGAR

TYPE:	GHOST-POISON
ABILITY:	LEVITATE
HEIGHT:	1.5m
WEIGHT:	40.5kg

This curious Pokémon lurks almost invisibly in the gloom of shadows. The air temperature will drop by at least 10°C when Gengar is hovering in the area.

072 MISDREAVUS

TYPE:	GHOST
ABILITY:	LEVITATE
HEIGHT:	0.7m
WEIGHT:	1kg

Misdreavus has a high-pitched shriek that pierces the air. It enjoys nothing better than creeping up on people late at night and then startling them with its eerie cry.

073 MISMAGIUS

TYPE:	GHOST
ABILITY:	LEVITATE
HEIGHT:	0.9m
WEIGHT:	4.4kg

Mismagius' chant-like howl can have a terrible effect on those that unlucky enough to hear it. Its victims are tortured by strange visions and splitting headaches.

074 MURKROW

TYPE:	DARK-FLYING
ABILITY:	INSOMNIA-SUPER LUCK
HEIGHT:	0.5m
WEIGHT:	2.1kg

Humans and Pokémon avoid Murkrow after nightfall. It is believed that the creature will bring bad luck to those that see it. Murkrow evolves into a Honchkrow.

075 HONCHKROW

TYPE:	DARK-FLYING
ABILITY:	INSOMNIA-SUPER LUCK
HEIGHT:	0.9m
WEIGHT:	27.3kg

Honchkrow is known to swarm with hoards of Murkrow flapping behind it. The Pokémon sends Murkrow to forage for its food, while it grooms itself in its nest.

076 GLAMEOW

TYPE:	NORMAL
ABILITY:	LIMBER-OWN TEMPO
HEIGHT:	0.5m
WEIGHT:	3.9kg

Glameow is a fickle creature that will flick out its claws to show its displeasure. The Pokémon's glare is bewitching enough to put its enemies into a mild hypnotic trance.

077 PURUGLY

TYPE:	NORMAL
ABILITY:	THICK FAT-OWN TEMPO
HEIGHT:	1m
WEIGHT:	43.8kg

Evolved from Glameow, Purugly has a domineering nature. It thinks nothing of marching into another Pokémon's nest and claiming the territory as its own.

078 GOLDEEN

TYPE:	WATER
ABILITY:	SWIFT SWIM-WATER VEIL
HEIGHT:	0.6m
WEIGHT:	15kg

Goldeen is a majestic Pokémon with proud eyes and an ivory horn. It swims by fluttering its gauzy tail fin as if it were a dress. Goldeen evolves into a Seaking.

079 SEAKING

TYPE:	WATER
ABILITY:	SWIFT SWIMMER-WATER VEIL
HEIGHT:	1.3m
WEIGHT:	39kg

Seaking makes a nest by hollowing out underwater rocks with its horn. Once it has laid a clutch of eggs it will guard the brood night and day, defending them with its life.

080 BARBOACH

TYPE:	WATER-GROUND
ABILITY:	OBLIVIOUS-ANTICIPATION
HEIGHT:	0.4m
WEIGHT:	1.9kg

Barboach slicks its body from whisker to tail in a slimy fluid. This makes sure that the Pokémon will be able to quickly squirm and slip away if grabbed by an enemy.

DAWN'S DASH

Our young Co-ordinator has got separated from her Pokémon! Pick the right path to lead Dawn back to her friends in time for her next contest.

MIME JR
SPOT THE DIFFERENCE

Only two of these Mime Jr are identical Pokémon.
Use your observation skills to study them all, then
circle the pair you think it might be.

MUTINY IN THE BOUNTY!

Ash and his friends are travelling to Floarama Town and Dawn's next contest. Unfortunately, a cold and ruthless Pokémon hunter stands in their way...

I t was an amazing sight. "What a beautiful field of flowers!" gushed Dawn. Rows and rows of stunning blooms stretched before them, as far as the eye could see. Ash was knocked out. "In the bright sunlight they look like they're on fire!"
Suddenly a shadow passed across the friends' heads. "What was that?" Dawn pressed a key on her Pokédex.

SALAMENCE
THE DRAGON POKÉMON

AS A RESULT OF A POWERFUL DESIRE TO FLY, SALAMENCE WERE ABLE TO TRIGGER THE CELLS IN THEIR BODY AND CAUSE THEM TO GROW WINGS.

Ash stared up at the sky. "Someone's riding it!" Brock pointed to a garden at the bottom of the hill, where they could just make out a girl tending some plants. A graceful Gardevoir Pokémon was floating at her side.

The Dragon Pokémon landed with a terrible thud in front of the girl. The girl screamed as a woman in a long, purple coat leapt off Salamence's back. She looked straight at the Gardevoir and smiled. "Target identified."

"Who're you?"

The mysterious rider didn't answer. Instead she pulled a Poké Ball from inside her coat. "Ariados, String Shot!"

Dawn and Ash gasped as a spider-like Bug Pokémon scuttled forwards, shooting thick webbing at the girl. It pinned its victim to a tree, binding her to the spot.

"She needs help!" cried Brock. Ash was already running. "C'mon!"

"I'll take Gardevoir," announced the stranger.

The girl's Pokémon tried to teleport itself, but it was no match for the intruder. She directed a wrist-mounted device at Gardevoir, hitting it with a strange beam.

"Now your beauty will be preserved for all eternity!" laughed the woman.

The girl cried out desperately as Gardevoir shimmered then set into a solid gold statue!

"Please help me get my Gardevoir back!" she begged. Ash clenched his fist in anger. "You can count on it!"

With Pikachu clutching on to his backpack, Ash sprinted down the track after the van. His only hope was to cut it off by scrambling vertically down the mountainside. He half-ran and half-somersaulted down, landing in a heap at the bottom.

The woman lifted her eye visor and smiled. "Mission accomplished. Transporting target now!"

A six wheel armoured van suddenly skidded into view. The group watched in disbelief as it released a base and a glass dome, trapping Gardevoir like a museum exhibit.

Within seconds, the gold figurine was loaded into the back of the van and whisked away. Salamence and its rider were soon soaring after it. Brock and Dawn dashed towards the tree where the girl, Melodi, was sobbing.

"Are you OK?" asked Ash, as his friends untied her.

The woman didn't appear to be listening. Ash shouted more loudly. "Give back Gardevoir!" At last she replied. "No can do… Go!" A fierce clawed Pokémon instantly appeared on the track. Ash glanced nervously down at his Pokédex… "I'd love to see Pikachu's other moves," said the woman. "So bring it on!"

Ash and Pikachu had made it just in the nick of time. "Quick Pikachu!" shouted Ash. "Use Thunderbolt!" Pikachu rocketed into the air, delivering a huge surge of lightning bolts onto the approaching van. The van kept moving. "It didn't do a thing," gasped Ash.

As the pair watched the van screech to a halt, the Salamence landed behind them. This time when she dismounted, the rider nodded towards Pikachu. "Impressive Thunderbolt. It should fetch a good price!" "Hey!" yelled Ash. "You can't just steal Pokémon!"

DRAPION
THE OGRE SCORP POKÉMON

ITS CLAWS GIVE OFF A DEADLY POISON, AND THEY ARE POWERFUL ENOUGH TO TURN AN AUTOMOBILE INTO SCRAP IRON.

With a quick hand movement, Ariados was dispatched to tie Ash to a nearby rock. "Pikachu!" thundered Ash. "You can't do that!"
He was too late. Pikachu was already being transported away.

As they watched safe from the distance, Team Rocket acknowledged their new rival.
"Let's knock her down a notch!" urged Meowth. Jessie agreed. "And once we're through working our magic she'll beg to work for us!"

Ash was fired up and ready to battle. He pointed at Pikachu and ordered, "Volt Tackle!" Pikachu began hurtling towards Drapion at an incredible speed, building current with every pace. The woman's initial surprise was replaced with pleasure. "Drapion, Dodge it!"
The vast Pokémon skilfully scuttled to the edge of the track, out of Pikachu's path. Unable to stop, Pikachu skidded to a halt at the stranger's feet. "Marvellous!" she beamed. "You're obviously worth quite a lot!"
Ash cried out helplessly as the woman directed her laser at Pikachu. Within a moment his beloved Pokémon was petrified in solid gold.
"He'll be fine," explained the woman in mock-concern. "I protect my investments!"

Melodi, Brock and Dawn sprinted round the bend in the road. "What happened?" asked Brock, trying to take in the scene.

Ash shouted in panic. "She got Gardevoir and Pikachu!"

Dawn hurled her Poké Ball. "Pachirisu use Spark to cut the thread!"

While Ash was being cut out of Ariados' webbing, further down the track the robber van was about to encounter a road block. All of a sudden the way ahead was shrouded in thick, grey fumes.

"Where'd this smoke come from?" coughed the driver. As the fog cleared, Jessie, James and Meowth were waiting to greet him.

"We're Team Rocket and we're in your face!" The driver wiped his eyes in disbelief as Meowth swaggered forward.

"Thanks for babysitting for Pikachu while we were out, but

we'll take over." Before their Pokémon could continue, Team Rocket were blasted to the ground. Meowth peered up to see Salamance looming above his head.

"A Meowth that can speak like a person?" smiled its rider. "I can sell that…"

James and Jessie unleashed their most battle-hardy Pokémon, but they were no match for this foe. Within seconds, the pair were lashed to a boulder.

"Meowth get here right now!" screeched Jessie. "Defend my honour!"

The mysterious thief laughed pityingly. "I'm afraid that Meowth's going to be tied up."

Before he could protest, Meowth was hit by the woman's potent lazer.

"No!" shrieked Jessie, watching her now gold Pokémon disappear into the armoured van. Suddenly Ash and his friends came tearing after the van. Ignoring Team Rocket's crabby cries for assistance, the group shielded their faces as a vast ship thundered into the skies above them.

They turned back when a motorcycle engine revved behind them – Officer Jenny!

"Were you following her too?" asked Brock.

Jenny nodded. "When I heard she was here I came as fast as I could."

"Who is she?" he questioned.

"Her name is J," answered Jenny. "And she's got a fearsome reputation as a Pokémon hunter!"

"Pokémon hunters can be hired to capture a certain Pokémon," explained Officer Jenny.
"But if they come across one of exceptional value they'll catch it anyway." Dawn was shocked.
"You mean for money?"
"They're ruthless!" nodded Jenny.
Ash could feel himself getting hotter and hotter.
"You OK?" asked Melodi.
"I can't stand it!" roared Ash.
"I'm gonna get my Pikachu back, or else!"

Still tied to a rock, Jessie and James were feeling pretty much the same way.
"I will not be out-nastied by a Team Rocket wannabe!" vowed Jessie.

Over on J's ship, Team Rocket's third member was trying to buy himself some time. One of the crew flicked a switch to unset Meowth's head, so he could video him.
"A talking Meowth is worth at least its weight in gold!" he grinned.

Meowth spotted his chance.
"Give me a second and I'll think of a Pokémon to get ya that's worth lots of dough!"

KIRLIA
THE EMOTION POKÉMON

KIRLIA USES THE HORNS ON ITS
HEAD TO AMPLIFY ITS PSYCHIC
POWERS AND WHEN THIS OCCURS
REALITY BECOMES WARPED AND
FUTURE EVENTS CAN BE SEEN.

"We can't chase after J," sighed Brock.
"But if we could only predict the next place
that she'll show up…"
Melodi pulled a Poké Ball out of her pocket.
"Maybe this could give us a hand."
"What's that?" asked Dawn, as a pale green
Pokémon materialised… Melodi crouched
next to Kirlia then showed her J's 'WANTED'
poster.

"This is the person that took Gardevoir,"
she said urgently. "We need to know where
she'll be going to hunt Pokémon next!"
Kirlia bowed its head and began to
meditate. Suddenly an image from the
future appeared. The group craned
to see a watermill next to a small hut.

"That place is at the edge of the forest!"
cried Officer Jenny. Ash was ready.
"So let's get over there right now!"

Ash and his friends rushed through the forest at breakneck speed. They arrived at the watermill just as J swooped in on Salamence. Yet another Pokémon was trapped in her evil beam.

Ash blew his cover and rushed towards the hunter.
"No!" shouted Officer Jenny. "It's too dangerous."
It was too late.
"J!" bellowed Ash. "Gimme back Pikachu now!"

J turned and smiled. "I guess I should commend you for discovering headquarters. Salamence, Hyper Beam!"
Salamence opened its jaws, knocking Ash back with a blaze of flames.

Officer Jenny turned to her loyal Pokémon, Arcanine. "Flamethrower!"
The two Pokémon exploded in a clash of fire, but Salamence's power was formidable. Arcanine was blasted through the air, dumping him at Jenny's feet.

"Well done Salamence," said J admiringly. "Let's go."

On cue, her armoured vehicle arrived to transport the latest Pokémon victim. J smiled cruelly as she and Salamence took to the skies.

Ash spotted his chance. He tore across the grass, dived under J's combat vehicle and clung on. As the van set off, the last thing he expected to find under there were fellow travellers. Unbelievably, Jessie and James were also clinging to the moving vehicle.

"That hunter hussy hauled off poor Meowth!" moaned James. Jessie was finding it hard to hold on.

"You gotta hang in there!" urged Ash.

Suddenly the van bumped over a dip, sending it careering into the air. As its wheels left the ground, Dawn and Brock caught a glimpse of its undercarriage. They both cried out at once. "There's Ash!" Dawn watched the van thunder towards its awaiting mother ship, then turned desperately to Officer Jenny.

"She's gonna get away again!" Jenny reached for her radio. "Engage tracking radar."

Suddenly the ship rose into the air.
"Where did Ash go?" asked Dawn.
"He's probably hanging on for dear life!" guessed Brock.

As soon as the coast was clear, Ash, Jessie and James crawled out from under the armoured van. They found themselves in the docking station of J's ship.
"Let's split up," said Ash.
"I do think that Twerp's right," agreed Jessie. Ash selected a Poké Ball then summoned some back-up.
"Aipom! Help me find Pikachu!"

While the others were scouring the ship, Meowth was trying to talk himself out of trouble. J had been brought to hear his money-making plan.
"I wanna work for you as a Pokétranslator!" he stuttered. "I can tell you what they're thinking!"
J and her henchman seemed interested. Meowth grinned,

his plan of stringing the hunter along until he could escape was working.
Somehow, J picked up on his thoughts. "No deal," she decided. "Freeze him again!"
As she turned to leave, J noticed that the door had been pushed open. "It appears we have intruders!"

Aipom had found the room where Meowth and Pikachu were being held, but now J was onto them. He scampered back to warn Ash.

Reunited, Ash and Aipom hurtled down the ship's corridors. Suddenly, an enormous purple beast leapt out of nowhere, seizing Ash in its claws.

"Let go!" screeched Ash, choking.
J stepped arrogantly around the corner. "Following me this far is brave indeed!"

Aipom sprung forward, causing J's Pokémon, Drapion, to temporarily lose its grip. "I'm getting Pikachu back right now!" promised Ash. He pulled out a Poké Ball. "Turtwig!"

Turtwig and Aipom used their most aggressive moves, but they were no match for Drapion. "Use Cross Poison!" commanded J.

The giant scorpion pounded Turtwig and Aipom with its overwhelming rays. At that moment Jessie and James came running towards them, followed by J's formidable troops.

"We're trapped!" cried Ash. Just in the nick of time, Aipom reached for a ventilation shaft above his trainer's head and tore off the grille.

While Turtwig took care of J's lackeys, the rest of the crew crawled down the air shaft as fast as they could. At last Aipom pushed open another grille. Ash, Jessie and James were in luck – they had climbed into J's Pokémon storage hangar! "Pikachu!" cried Ash, spotting his friend.

Jessie was horrified. "What have they done?" Every Pokémon in the hangar was still set in gold. Only Meowth was free from the neck up. "Quick!" he called. "Flick that lever before my head falls off!" As soon as the Pokémon were restored, Ash hugged Pikachu as tight as he could.

"Not so fast!" cried a voice. The group turned round just as J's right hand man hurled a Poké Ball towards them. "Golbat! Steelwing now!" "Use Volt Tackle!" yelled Ash. The bat-like creature flew at Pikachu, but Ash's Pokémon charged him at breathtaking speed. As Golbat recoiled on the floor, his master ordered him in a second time. "Supersonic, go!"

Ash had
to think quickly.
"Pikachu, Thunderbolt!"
Pikachu fired his electric
barbs, knocking down Golbat
but also scorching a hole in
the ship's wall. All pressure
was instantly lost! The enemies
clung onto whatever they could
in a desperate struggle to
avoid being sucked out.
Using one arm to secure
himself to a table leg, Ash
recalled Turtwig and Aipom.
It was time to summon Staravia.

"Tell
Officer Jenny
where we are!"
The sharp-eyed Flying
Pokémon winged its way
through the opening and
soared off into the distance.

While the group struggled for
their lives, J's captain notified
his mistress of the damage to
Hangar number three.

"Such a nuisance!" spat J.
"Jettison the hangar."
The captain started to sweat.
"But some of our people are on
board."
J's eyes narrowed. "Who cares?
Just do it!"
"R-right!" wavered the captain,
sending the damaged chamber
reeling towards the ground.

Dawn stared through her binoculars in horror. "They're going to hit the ground hard!" Melodi closed her eyes and concentrated all her powers of telepathy. Her Gardevoir was one of the Pokémon in that hangar! "Teleport!" she whispered. Just as the hangar crashed to Earth in a terrible explosion, Gardevoir teleported its passengers onto the ground. Ash opened his eyes. "Pikachu we've been saved!" Brock and Dawn ran over to their friends while Officer Jenny tossed a rope around J's stunned crew.

"You men are all under arrest!" she shouted.

"I still can't get over J," sighed Dawn as they walked away. "To think people like that actually exist!"
"Officer Jenny will catch her one of these days," promised Brock. As J's ship disappeared into the distance, he shook his head. "Nobody gets away with that kind of thing forever."
Ash nodded sadly. "It's hard, but we just have to know that's true."

After encountering the ruthless Pokémon hunter J, our heroes will once again make their way to Floarama Town. But after this experience, they'll never be the same again…

POKÉMON TIME CHALLENGE

Pokémon trainers have to be super-quick, both in body and mind. Put your brain's rapid reactions to the test by seeing how many words you can form out of the phrase below in under three minutes!

ASH BATTLES WITH PIKACHU

1. ....
2. ....
3. ....
4. ....
5. ....
6. ....
7. ....
8. ....
9. ....
10. ....
11. ....
12. ....
13. ....
14. ....
15. ....
16. ....
17. ....
18. ....
19. ....

20. ....
21. ....
22. ....
23. ....
24. ....
25. ....
26. ....
27. ....
28. ....
29. ....
30. ....
31. ....
32. ....
33. ....
34. ....
35. ....
36. ....
37. ....
38. ....

39. ....
40. ....
41. ....
42. ....
43. ....
44. ....
45. ....
46. ....
47. ....
48. ....
49. ....
50. ....
51. ....
52. ....
53. ....
54. ....
55. ....
56. ....
57. ....

BATTLE MOVES

These Pokémon are giving everything they've got! Study each set of combat moves, then draw in the battling Pokémon that should go in next.

081 WHISCASH

TYPE:	WATER-GROUND
ABILITY:	OBLIVIOUS-ANTICIPATION
HEIGHT:	0.9m
WEIGHT:	23.6kg

Barboach evolves into a Whiscash. The Pokémon fiercely guards its territory. If an intruder approaches it uses its whiskers to set off tremors that can travel three miles.

082 CHINGLING

TYPE:	PSYCHIC
ABILITY:	LEVITATE
HEIGHT:	0.2m
WEIGHT:	0.6kg

Chingling makes a strange ringing sound every time it hops. It emits screams when it agitates an orb at the back of its throat. The cry is regularly used to deafen its foes.

083 CHIMECHO

TYPE:	PSYCHIC
ABILITY:	LEVITATE
HEIGHT:	0.6m
WEIGHT:	1kg

Chimecho sends its adversaries spinning in all directions by making the air shudder with the force of its cries. It communicates by blending seven shrieking noises.

084 STUNKY

TYPE:	POISON-DARK
ABILITY:	STENCH-AFTERMATH
HEIGHT:	0.4m
WEIGHT:	19.2kg

This smelly Pokémon wards off its foes by squirting a vile liquid from its rear end. The fluid creates an appalling stench that will linger in the air for over 24 hours.

085 SKUNTANK

TYPE:	POISON-DARK
ABILITY:	STENCH-AFTERMATH
HEIGHT:	1m
WEIGHT:	38kg

Skuntank's intense smell has intensified during its evolution from Stunky. Attackers are instantly repelled as it sprays them with a putrid shower from the tip of its tail.

086 MEDITITE

TYPE:	FIGHTING-PSYCHIC
ABILITY:	PURE POWER
HEIGHT:	0.6m
WEIGHT:	11.2kg

Meditite permits itself to eat only one berry a day. This hunger balances it spirit and makes it mind sharp and full of increased insight. Meditite evolves into a Medicham.

087 MEDICHAM

TYPE:	FIGHTING-PSYCHIC
ABILITY:	PURE POWER
HEIGHT:	1.3m
WEIGHT:	31.5kg

Medicham trains in meditation to the highest level, giving it the ability it to refine its sixth sense. The Pokémon's movements are both graceful, calm and elegant.

088 BRONZOR

TYPE:	STEEL-PSYCHIC
ABILITY:	LEVITATE-HEATPROOF
HEIGHT:	0.5m
WEIGHT:	60.5kg

Implements shaped like Bronzor were discovered in ancient tombs. When placed under an X-ray, no trace of the Pokémon appears. Bronzor evolves into a Bronzong.

089 BRONZONG

TYPE:	STEEL-PSYCHIC
ABILITY:	LEVITATE-HEATPROOF
HEIGHT:	1.3m
WEIGHT:	187kg

Humans are in awe of this Pokémon's mysterious ability to summon rain clouds. Once a Bronzong was dug up on a building site after a 2,000 year sleep.

090 PONYTA

TYPE:	FIRE
ABILITY:	RUN AWAY-FLASH FIRE
HEIGHT:	1m
WEIGHT:	30kg

Ponyta's mane and tail blaze out within an hour of being born. Its fiery flash of hair makes a striking impression on new challengers. Ponyta evolves into a Rapidash.

091 RAPIDASH

TYPE:	FIRE
ABILITY:	RUN AWAY-FLASH FIRE
HEIGHT:	1.7m
WEIGHT:	95kg

When Rapidash accelerates into a full gallop, it can be easily mistaken for a burning arrow. The fiery Pokémon can streak past at a speed of at least 240 km/h.

092 BONSLY

TYPE:	ROCK
ABILITY:	STURDY-ROCK HEAD
HEIGHT:	0.5m
WEIGHT:	15kg

Bonsly is most content in parched areas. Although it looks as if it is crying most of the time, the Pokémon deliberately leaks water to adjust the fluid levels in its body.

093 SUDOWOODO

TYPE:	ROCK
ABILITY:	STURDY-ROCK HEAD
HEIGHT:	1.2m
WEIGHT:	38kg

Despite its tree-like appearance, Sudowoodo's body mass is closer to rocks and stone. The Pokémon is exceptionally weak in water. It evolves from Bonsly.

094 MIME JR

TYPE:	PSYCHIC
ABILITY:	SOUNDPROOF-FILTER
HEIGHT:	0.6m
WEIGHT:	13kg

Mime Jr confuses its enemies by mimicking their behaviour. Once copied, the foe cannot tear its eyes away from Mime Jr. It is most effective in busy crowds of people.

095 MR MIME

TYPE:	PSYCHIC
ABILITY:	SOUNDPROOF-FILTER
HEIGHT:	1.3m
WEIGHT:	54.5kg

Evolved from Mime Jr, Mr Mime is a pantomime expert. It uses skilful miming gestures to create invisible but solid walls to stop enemies in their tracks.

096 HAPPINY

TYPE:	NORMAL
ABILITY:	NATURAL CURE-SERENE GRACE
HEIGHT:	0.6m
WEIGHT:	24.4kg

Gentle Happiny carries a white, egg-shaped rock in its belly pouch. It likes to give the rock away to its friends. Happiny evolves into a Chansey and then a Blissey.

097 CHANSEY

TYPE:	NORMAL
ABILITY:	NATURAL CURE-SERENE GRACE
HEIGHT:	1.1m
WEIGHT:	34.6kg

It is generally believed that Chansey brings happiness to those it meets. It will generously share its smooth round eggs with those that are hurt or injured.

098 BLISSEY

TYPE:	NORMAL
ABILITY:	NATURAL CURE-SERENE GRACE
HEIGHT:	1.5m
WEIGHT:	46.8kg

Blissey can sense if there is sadness troubling anyone around it. It is a kind-hearted creature that is highly proficient at nursing sick Pokémon back to health.

099 CLEFFA

TYPE:	NORMAL
ABILITY:	CUTE CHARM-MAGIC GUARD
HEIGHT:	0.3m
WEIGHT:	3.0kg

This Pokémon's silhouette looks like a star. When it approaches, it is believed to ride on the back of a shooting star. Cleffa evolves into a Clefairy and then a Clefable.

100 CLEFAIRY

TYPE:	NORMAL
ABILITY:	CUTE CHARM-MAGIC GUARD
HEIGHT:	7.5m
WEIGHT:	0.6kg

Clefairy is a hugely popular Pokémon, due to its adorable nature. No one is certain where it lives, but it is thought to dwell peacefully on quiet mountain tops.

You'll need to have all your felt tips or crayons ready to colour in this picture of our hero Ash and his pals! Use the number key to help you choose the right colour for each section of this cool scene.

COOKING UP A SWEET STORY!

As the Floarama contest draws near, Ash and Pikachu are providing Dawn with some formidable training partners! Now the friends need to watch out for Team Rocket...

"Piplup, use Bubblebeam!" ordered Dawn. The little Pokémon directed a barrage of blue hydro-bolts at Pikachu. Ash looked at Pikachu. "Dodge!" Pikachu neatly back-flipped out of danger, landing at Ash's feet. Brock was impressed by the training session. "Piplup is in tip-top shape!"
As she beckoned for her Pokémon to return, Dawn couldn't resist a smile. "Piplup,

you take a nice long rest."
Within seconds, the young co-ordinator was ready to battle again. "Pachirisu, you're up next." She ordered her Electric-type Pokémon to attempt a Discharge. Pachirisu leapt to a great height, then channelled a beam of sparks down at Pikachu.

Ash held out his palm. "Just stay put!"
Pikachu expertly used his tail to deflect the power surge.
"Hmm," mused Dawn. "I was afraid that Discharge wouldn't work on Pikachu."
Ash chuckled. "Now it's our turn. Pikachu, Thunderbolt!"

Pikachu delivered a violent Thunderbolt that Pachirisu only just managed to dodge.
"That was an amazing Thunderbolt!"

Ash turned round to see a girl kneel down and admire Pikachu.
"Wow," she cooed.
"If only I could borrow you!"
Ash scratched his head. "Sorry, I'm not following ya?"
The girl blushed. "I'm Theresa, and just down this road I run a cake shop with my Aunt Abigail."

As the friends followed Theresa back to her café, they talked some more.

"My aunt has been making cakes for years with her partner, a Pikachu called Sugar," she explained.

"But something strange happened and Sugar disappeared!"
With a bake-off contest taking place three days from now, Theresa asked if Pikachu would pose as Sugar to help Aunt Abigail get through it.
"Won't she be able to tell the difference?" asked Ash.
Theresa shook her head.
"All your Pikachu has to do is scratch its head with its tail every once in a while."

67

Theresa, Ash, Dawn and Brock stood nervously behind the door of the cake shop. If the plan was going to work, Pikachu needed to put in the performance of his life.

"Welcome!" called Aunt Abigail as the entrance bell rang. The old lady did a double-take. There, below the counter, was an adorable Pikachu that looked just like her missing Sugar! "You've come back home?" she cried in disbelief.

Theresa led her new friends into the shop. "Isn't is great? These guys found Sugar!" Aunt Abigail was overwhelmed. "Thank you so much!"

While Dawn, Ash and Brock enjoyed tea on the house, Pikachu displayed his awesome acting skills. "It's working like a charm!" said Brock.

"Sure is!" grinned Theresa. "Aunt Abby's back to her old self again."

The group watched as Abigail led Pikachu out the door. Theresa clapped her hands in delight. "She's going to buy supplies for her famous contest-winning cake!"

Outside, Team Rocket were onto their latest moneymaking scheme. Jessie, James and Meowth were each loaded with crates of berries.

"Those Contest Pokémon gotta eat," sniggered Meowth. "So we'll bring the treat!" A thunderbolt suddenly split the sky.

"Wow!" gasped James. "That was Class A electronics!" Meowth stopped. "Looked like Pike-power to me." Team Rocket dumped their berries and crept forward to take a closer look. In the forest, Pikachu was helping a little old lady blast berries off the trees!

"Thank you Sugar," she said sweetly, "You've turned them the perfect shade of brown."

Jessie rustled the bush nosily. "That has to be the Pika-Twerp!" James shrugged. "Why's the name Sugar being bandied about?" Back at the shop, Theresa served up some delicious cakes.

"Using Pikachu's Thunderbolt is the best method for getting that unique roasted berry flavour!" she smiled.

Ash felt a little uneasy without his Pokémon. "I think I'm gonna look for him!"

Unaware she was being spied on, Abigail prepared to head home.

"This is plenty!" she said, smiling at her basketful of sweet berries. Before she could take a single step, Jessie, James and Meowth burst out of the undergrowth. "You and the berries may leave," shouted James. "But the Pikachu stays put!"

"Heaven's sakes!" declared Aunt Abigail. "Who are you?" Jessie was just too vain to let this opportunity pass her by. "We're Team Rocket and we're in your face!"

At that moment, Theresa led her friends into the berry orchard.

Ash started at the sight of his old enemies. "We gotta help out Abigail!" cried Ash.

"Hold on!" said Theresa firmly. "My aunt takes care of herself!" Against Ash's instincts, the gang held back.

Aunt Abigail stayed calm. "I'm sorry, but you can't have Sugar."
Meowth looked over at Jessie and laughed. "It's crunch time!"

Jessie slung a Poké Ball into the air. "Seviper, let's go!"

Team Rocket's Seviper, seethed and coiled towards Pikachu.

"Pikachu!" called Aunt Abigail. "Move towards the tree on the right!" The Pokémon obeyed, even though it looked like a retreat.

Jessie rubbed her hands together impatiently. "All right," she hissed. "Use Bite Seviper!"
As Seviper lunged at Pikachu, Abigail gave her next command. "Now, Thunderbolt straight up!"

A bolt tore into the tree above Pikachu severing a spotted berry. The berry dropped like a lead weight, striking a direct hit on Seviper's head.

"Those Aspear berries are as hard as rocks!" marvelled Brock. Ash was knocked-out. "What a strategy!"

Aunt Abigail was in total control now. "All right Sugar, use Thunderbolt on Seviper!" In one swift move, the Poison Pokémon and its hapless masters were catapulted into oblivion.

As Team Rocket tumbled over the horizon, the old lady stepped forward to praise Pikachu. "Sugar, you were wonderful!"

Ash ran out to congratulate Aunt Abigail, convinced that only a Pokémon trainer could have pulled off such sharp battle moves.

"She's competed in the Grand Festival," Theresa proudly announced. "I see you haven't lost any of your battling skills Auntie!"

"It's all ancient history now," said Abigail. "You're going for the Sinnoh League aren't you Ash?"

"Yeah!" replied Ash. "My next battle's gonna be at the Eterna Gym."

Aunt Abigail had a twinkle in her eye. "Would you care to battle with me then?"

Ash was speechless.

"Of course I'll be working with Sugar," she continued. "How about it?"

Theresa and Ash exchanged worried glances.

"I'm not sure that it's a good idea Auntie," said Theresa. But the old lady refused to take no for an answer.

"I'm sure you're training hard for your next bout. And that's just what this would be."

Ash was left with no choice. "Uh… I guess."

Theresa reluctantly stepped forward. "The battle between Ash and Aunt Abigail is about to get underway!"

Dawn looked nervously at Brock. "I don't like this one bit." Abigail gave Ash a cheery smile. "So what Pokémon will you be using today?" Ash turned his head away and tried to think. He totally didn't want to battle against Pikachu, but if he withdrew Abigail was going to

suspect something was up! Reluctantly, he turned back to his opponent. "OK Aipom, I choose you!"
Aipom took his place on the field, and then spotted Pikachu.

Confused, he waved his tail at his master.
"A battle is a battle!" urged Ash.
"I'm sorry Ash," whispered Theresa. "Begin!"
Abigail signalled to Pikachu. "Sugar, Dash now!"

As Pikachu raced towards them, Ash ordered a Double Team. His Pokémon suddenly replicated itself, surrounding Pikachu with a ring of Aipoms.
"Jump Sugar!" instructed Abigail. "Then use Thunderbolt, straight down!"

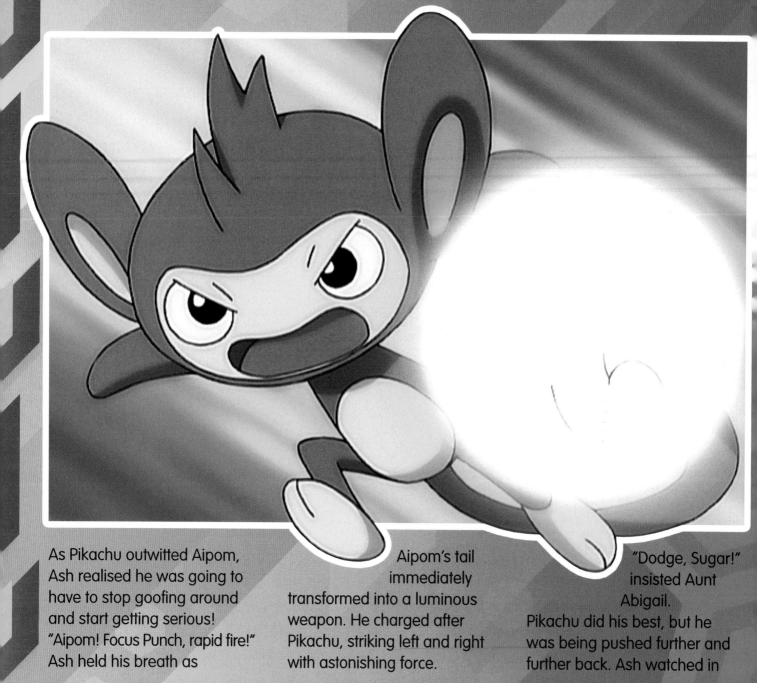

As Pikachu outwitted Aipom, Ash realised he was going to have to stop goofing around and start getting serious! "Aipom! Focus Punch, rapid fire!" Ash held his breath as

Aipom's tail immediately transformed into a luminous weapon. He charged after Pikachu, striking left and right with astonishing force.

"Dodge, Sugar!" insisted Aunt Abigail.
Pikachu did his best, but he was being pushed further and further back. Ash watched in

terror as Aipom moved in for the knock-out. He couldn't bear to see his friend being struck down by his own command!

Aunt Abigail suddenly stepped in front of Pikachu, deflecting the blow with her skirts. "Enough!" Ash was relieved, but totally confused. "I'm impressed!" said Aunt Abigail graciously. "No sense going on since we've lost."
"But why?" stuttered Ash. Aunt Abigail simply smiled. "You're a good boy. Now Sugar,

shall we go?" The youngsters stared after her in stunned silence as she set off for the cake shop.

That evening, Aunt Abigail and Pikachu started baking the cake for the contest. Theresa was bubbling with excitement, but Ash felt uneasy.
"I'm worried that when your Aunt learns the truth, she's gonna be sad," he admitted. "We can't just leave Pikachu here with her forever," added Dawn.

"Please don't worry," pleaded Theresa. "After she wins first prize in the bake-off she's going to a feel better, then you can go!" Ash shook his head. "I think she quit our battle early because of how much Pika, I mean 'Sugar', means to her."
Theresa's face dropped. "But Ash!"
"I really wanted to help your Aunt get over being sad, but we're not telling the truth!" Ash turned to Brock and Dawn. "I've got to set the record straight once and for all!"

Aunt Abigail looked fondly at Ash's Pokémon. "This is actually your Pikachu, is that right?" Brock, Dawn and Theresa rushed onto the veranda.
"So you already knew?" gasped Theresa.
Aunt Abigail nodded. "Pikachu did a fine job with the berries, but Sugar never did it in exactly the same way."
"Well whaddya know," shrugged Ash.

"The truth is, we actually know why Sugar disappeared," Abigail went on, taking an Aspear berry out of her basket. Theresa sighed as her aunt explained how Sugar's Thunderbolt didn't have the power to crack the berries open that they needed for their cakes. "Then Sugar left," she interrupted. "To go find some way to do what my aunt had asked."

"Thank you," said Abigail. "I feel much better having spent a day with Pikachu."
"Glad ta help," replied Ash.

Before he could say another word a robotic arm swooped onto the veranda, grabbing Pikachu in one calculated stroke!

It was Team Rocket, and they had snatched Pikachu in their berry-shaped pod-craft! Jessie and Meowth laughed cruelly as James pushed the Pokémon into a cage.

"Quick Pikachu, Thunderbolt!" yelled Ash, sprinting after the pod.
"Did you think we'd let you zap us to kingdom come?" called James.
Ash made a desperate leap onto the back of the craft.

"You're not getting away!" Aunt Abigail looked seriously at Theresa. "Come on. Let's get after them in the van."
As the pod motored forwards, Ash pulled out a Poké Ball.
"Staravia! Wing Attacks, non stop!" The bird Pokémon butted Team Rocket's craft again and again. It was having no effect.
"Let 'em try this!" shouted Ash.
"Maximum power Aerial Ace, let's go!"

Staravia nosedived towards the vehicle at lightning speed, but Team Rocket steered over a cliff edge. Ash was sent tumbling into the mud. Before it could impact, a robotic arm punched Staravia out of the skies.

As Ash called Staravia back, the others scrambled out of the van. "My old vehicle won't make it down that cliff!" cried Theresa. "What do we do now?" exclaimed Dawn, as Team Rocket sped into the distance. Aunt Abigail was furious. "The nerve of those three. You will *not* have Pikachu!" As if obeying orders, the night sky suddenly turned white.

A flash of blinding light stopped the podcraft in its tracks. "Looks like a Thunderbolt!" gasped Ash. Dawn craned to see. "It can't be Pikachu cos it's coming from the outside!" "What awesome power!" said Brock. Ash had seen this many times before. "It's a Raichu."

"Raichu?" Aunt Abigail called into the breeze. "Sugar, could it really be *you*?" "Sugar?" everybody burst out at the same time.

Theresa finally understood. "Sugar must have evolved into Raichu!" Before they could greet the long-lost Pokémon, Team Rocket's pod-craft reversed and ploughed after it.

The Raichu was ready, smashing the pod's robotic arms to smithereens. "That was a Focus Punch!" squealed Dawn.

The Raichu skilfully grabbed Pikachu's cage, then leapt out of the hole in the craft.

"That was some Focus Punch!" gushed Dawn.
Ash greeted his beloved Pikachu. "Thanks Raichu!"

Theresa grinned proudly. "Sugar's been learning all sorts of new things!" Aunt Abigail clenched her fists. "Sugar! Go rescue the Pikachu they stole!" Sugar furrowed his brow, then began thumping the craft with killer punches.

Inside, Jessie and James were starting to lose their nerve. Meowth shrugged it off, pointing at the reinforced walls. "I put everything I know into making this machine!" In seconds, Sugar had beaten through the armour like it was paper! Team Rocket looked aghast at the gaping hole in their cockpit wall. "I say we rethink this!" screamed James, shooting Meowth an angry look.

Everyone smiled as Pikachu pipped and squeaked his thanks to Raichu.

Abigail clasped her hands together in delight. "And now Sugar is going to use a Thunderbolt, just like old times!" Raichu bounded into the sky with a terrible force that shook the ground under their feet. Suddenly an incredible electric charge channelled out of his cheeks, straight into the side of the pod-craft.

The spectators gasped as the vehicle exploded in a shower of smoke and flame, sending Team Rocket somersaulting into the air.

"Never again will we build another machine in-house!" screeched Jessie.

"Think of the money we saved," James hollered back. Meowth furiously punched the air as the unhappy trio sailed into the distance. "You know how much flying costs these days?" Ash laughed. Team Rocket were blasting off again, and it looked like they wouldn't be back for some time!

"And here we are!" Everyone clapped as Aunt Abigail placed her delicious cake on the table. Ash licked his lips. "If that isn't a first prize-winning cake I don't know what is!"

"It's filled with those Aspear Berries," explained Theresa. "Then they were pulverised using Focus Punch!" Aunt Abigail cut generous slices and passed them round. "Yum-my!" said Dawn.

"There's something about those Aspear Berries that just hits the spot," agreed Brock.

"You're all very kind," beamed Abigail.

"Sugar learned Focus Punch just to open those berries," giggled Theresa. "...and now look!"

Brock bowed his head. "Sugar, you were great!"

Dawn was inspired. "Now I know in my next contest I'll win first prize too!"

"Yeah!" encouraged Ash. "Keep thinking that way and you'll *have* to win it!"

A good-hearted woman and her Raichu have shown our heroes how affection can work miracles. Now Dawn is more excited than ever about her next Pokémon Contest!

101 CLEFABLE

TYPE:	NORMAL
ABILITY:	CUTE CHARM-MAGIC GUARD
HEIGHT:	1.3m
WEIGHT:	40kg

Clefable is rarely sighted by people. The reclusive Pokémon is said to be drawn by the power of the full moon, leading to play around the edge of deserted lakes.

102 CHATOT

TYPE:	NORMAL-FLYING
ABILITY:	KEEN EYE-TANGLED FEET
HEIGHT:	0.5m
WEIGHT:	1.9kg

Chatot is a master at imitating human speech. It keeps rhythm by flicking its tail like a metronome. When groups of Chatot gather, they all learn the same phrases.

103 PICHU

TYPE:	ELECTRIC
ABILITY:	STATIC
HEIGHT:	0.3m
WEIGHT:	2kg

Pichu is an electric Pokémon, but its small cheeks mean that it doesn't have the capacity to store much charge yet. It evolves into a Pikachu and then a Raichu.

104 PIKACHU

TYPE:	ELECTRIC
ABILITY:	STATIC
HEIGHT:	0.4m
WEIGHT:	6kg

Pikachu live together in forests. Its developed cheek pouches are used to store high levels of electricity. This sparky Pokémon can form loyal friendships.

105 RAICHU

TYPE:	ELECTRIC
ABILITY:	STATIC
HEIGHT:	0.8m
WEIGHT:	30kg

If there is too much electricity in its body, Raichu will turn aggressive. It discharges the power through end of its tail. The air around Raichu can flash and snap.

106 HOOTHOOT

TYPE:	NORMAL-FLYING
ABILITY:	INSOMNIA-KEEN EYE
HEIGHT:	0.7m
WEIGHT:	21.2kg

This curious Pokémon will always perch on one, solitary foot. Even when challenged by an attacker, it will not brace itself with both feet. It evolves into a Noctowl.

107 NOCTOWL

TYPE:	NORMAL-FLYING
ABILITY:	INSOMNIA-KEEN EYE
HEIGHT:	1.6m
WEIGHT:	40.8kg

Noctowl's unique strength is its super-powerful eyesight. Its large red eyes can pick out objects from almost any distance, as long as there is the barest amount of light.

108 SPIRITOMB

TYPE:	GHOST-DARK
ABILITY:	PRESSURE
HEIGHT:	1m
WEIGHT:	108kg

This Pokémon was formed by 108 spirits. It was bound to a fissure in an odd keystone as punishment for misdeeds committed 500 years ago.

109 Gible

TYPE:	DRAGON-GROUND
ABILITY:	SAND VEIL
HEIGHT:	0.7m
WEIGHT:	20.5kg

At one time, Gible lived in the tropics. To avoid the cold, it seeks out caves warmed by geothermal heat. It pounces to catch prey that stray too close to its home.

110 GABITE

TYPE:	DRAGON-GROUND
ABILITY:	SAND VEIL
HEIGHT:	1.4m
WEIGHT:	56kg

It is believed that medicine made from Gabite's scales will cure every type of illness. It likes to dig up and hoard gems in its nest. Gabite is evolved from Gible.

111 GARCHOMP

TYPE:	DRAGON-GROUND
ABILITY:	SAND VEIL
HEIGHT:	1.9m
WEIGHT:	95kg

Garchomp can fold up its body and extend its wings like a jet plane. Evolved from a Gabite, this Pokémon can fly at super sonic speeds. No prey can escape it.

112 MUNCHLAX

TYPE:	NORMAL
ABILITY:	PICKUP-THICK FAT
HEIGHT:	0.6m
WEIGHT:	105kg

Munchlax needs to eats the equivalent of its weight in food at least once a day. It gulps down great mouthfuls without swallowing. It hides food under its long hair.

113 SNORLAX

TYPE:	NORMAL
ABILITY:	IMMUNITY-THICK FAT
HEIGHT:	2.1m
WEIGHT:	460kg

Snorlax's enormous stomach can digest any type of food. It will happily eat mouldy or rotten snacks without noticing. Snorlax is evolved from a Munchlax.

114 UNOWN

TYPE:	PSYCHIC
ABILITY:	LEVITATE
HEIGHT:	0.5m
WEIGHT:	5kg

Unown is shaped like an ancient hieroglyphic. There is a huge mystery about which came first – language or Unown. The Pokémon has not evolved into any forms.

115 RIOLU

TYPE:	FIGHTING
ABILITY:	STEADFAST-INNER FOCUS
HEIGHT:	0.7m
WEIGHT:	20.2kg

Riolu uses the aura around its body to show others whether it is sad or frightened. It has the power to climb three mountains and cross two canyons in a single night.

116 LUCARIO

TYPE:	FIGHTING-STEEL
ABILITY:	STEADFAST-INNER FOCUS
HEIGHT:	1.2m
WEIGHT:	54kg

Evolved from Riolu, Lucario has the ability to understand human speech. It also senses other creatures' auras and uses them to read their thoughts and movements.

117 WOOPER

TYPE:	WATER-GROUND
ABILITY:	DAMP-WATER ABSORB
HEIGHT:	0.4m
WEIGHT:	8.5kg

Wooper can only be found in water. When it needs to sleep, it half buries itself in the mud at the bottom of its river or lake. The Pokémon evolves into a Quagsire.

118 QUAGSIRE

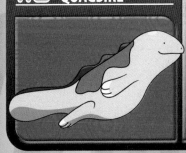

TYPE:	WATER-GROUND
ABILITY:	DAMP-WATER ABSORB
HEIGHT:	1.4m
WEIGHT:	75kg

Quagsire is slow and cumbersome. The Pokémon is content to lurk at the bottom of a riverbed, waiting for prey to stray into its mouth. It is rarely spotted whilst moving.

119 WINGULL

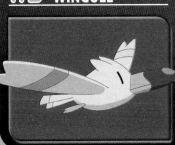

TYPE:	WATER-FLYING
ABILITY:	KEEN EYE
HEIGHT:	0.6m
WEIGHT:	9.5kg

Wingull chooses to nest safe above its prey on sea cliff faces. When it is travelling against the tide, it soars to great heights above the water. It evolves into a Pelipper.

120 PELIPPER

TYPE:	WATER-FLYING
ABILITY:	KEEN EYE
HEIGHT:	1.2m
WEIGHT:	28kg

Pelipper is known for its distinctive beak. The Pokémon fishes by flapping above the waves and dipping its bill in the sea. It scoops up water and prey in one quick dip.

DOUBLE TEAM AIPOM

When Ash asks Aipom to do Double Team, Team Rocket better watch out! Aipom has the pests surrounded in seconds, but can you count how many times he's duplicated himself using this knock-out move?

HOW MANY CAN YOU COUNT?

CROSSWORDS WITH BROCK

Can you help Brock crack the clues and complete this crossword challenge? See how quickly you can fill in all the right answers. Good luck, some of these are pretty tough!

DOWN

1. Buneary evolves into this cautious Pokémon.
2. Police woman that sends Brock's heart fluttering.
3. Snover likes to live in these conditions.
4. Ash must win eight of these if he wants to compete in the Sinnoh League.
5. Pikachu's next evolution.

ACROSS

1. A Electric Pokémon that generates sparks through its claws, and evolved to Luxray.
2. The flowery city hosting Dawn's next contest.
3. An agile climber, this Pokémon evolves into Monferno.
4. Budew is th is colour.
5. Ash's last name.
6. The electronic index that no Pokémon Trainer can do without.

ALL DRESSED UP
WITH SOMEWHERE TO GO!

On their way to the Eterna Gym, our heroes take a break to discover a Pokémon Dress-up Contest. Ash, Dawn and Brock are about to witness Sinnoh's most exciting competition in years...

Ash settled into his seat at the TV studio. Suddenly the audience went crazy as *Sinnoh Now* host Rhonda walked onto the stage. "Welcome to the Pokémon Dress-up Contest!" she beamed.
"Cool!" whispered Ash. "Can't wait to see it!"

"Pokémon and trainers are hoping to win our grand prize," continued Rhonda."An exquisite egg specially selected for these festivities!"
The presenter had to wait for the crowd to stop clapping before she could go on.
"Please welcome our judges Nurse Joy, Officer Jenny and

main man Mr Sukizo!"
Brock sighed as Mr Sukizo entered arm-in-arm with his co-judges. "What I wouldn't give to be in his place!"
Dawn giggled with excitement. "Sinnoh's Dress-up contest is so popular it ranks number one in the ratings every season!"

Rhonda whisked round and pointed to a giant flat screen above the stage.
"Let's get to our registration-cam and see how things are going out front!"
The screen showed a room filled with contestants waiting to take part. Suddenly a woman in a cowgirl outfit filled the screen.
"I intend to win this contest with talent as well as style!" she boasted, preening for the camera.
Back in the studio, Rhonda coughed nervously. "But only Pokémon can enter…"
"No way, no fair!" cried the woman. Suddenly her sunglasses slipped, revealing Jessie's pouting face.
"Don't I know you?" asked Rhonda. "You look like another actress we had a run-in with before…"
James quickly covered for his crony. "You must be thinking of someone else!
Anyway, my Mime Jr's going to win the whole shebang!"

Jessie dangled her Pokémon in front of the camera.
"The real winner will be my Meowth!"
Rhonda decided that it was time for a commercial break.

"The awesome feeling that you get when your Pokémon egg finally hatches is something you just can't put into words," remembered Brock.

Ash grinned. "Sounds pretty cool!"

"Yup!" Now Brock pictured himself beside Officer Jenny and Nurse Joy. "And girls love a guy with an egg!"

Ash sped off ahead. "Here's to winning!"

"I'm right behind ya buddy!" puffed Brock.

"Hold it boys!" shouted Dawn.

Ash, Pikachu and Brock all skidded to a halt. "Wh-what?"

"You need to choose which Pokémon to enter first!" she explained. "Rule is there's only one Pokémon per Co-ordinator.

Ash burst out of the studio and started running down the corridor.

"Where are you going in such a rush?" asked Dawn.

"I gotta hurry and register!" he puffed.

"I'd love to win that Pokémon Egg too, ya know?"

Brock started to dream. "That would be great…"

"A Pokémon egg," imagined Dawn. "I want one!"

In a Dress-up Contest, Pokémon are judged on how well they can imitate other Pokémon. Ash was finding it almost impossible to decide which of his Pokémon was up to the job! He lined them all up in the corridor.

"Let's see," he muttered.

"Maybe Aipom?"

He imagined Aipom in a Turtwig costume, but he ended up looking totally wrong.

"Man!" cried Ash.

Pikachu suddenly started squeaking and jumping on the spot. He wanted to give it a shot. Ash kneeled down next to him.

"It's not enough to change your colour a little bit so that you look like a Raichu or Pichu remember."

Pikachu immediately closed his eyes and wrinkled his mouth. He looked just like Wobbuffet! In seconds he stretched his face into one Pokémon and then another.

"If you can get people to guess who you are just by facial expressions, you'll make big points!" gasped Brock.

"Pikachu!" cried Ash. "You're in!"

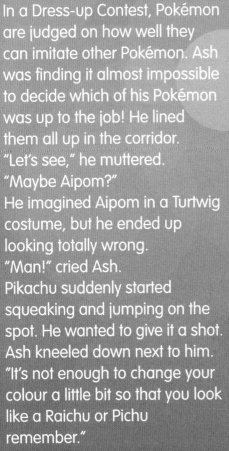

Once Dawn had teamed up with Piplup and Brock had chosen Croagunk, the gang were ready to compete. Rhonda had the crowd buzzing with excitement by the time the first contestant stepped onto the stage.

"Wow!" she purred. "It takes some skill to do an imitation of the legendary Pokémon Suicine!" The judges voted which performances deserved to go through to the next round. Many got voted off, but places in the final were disappearing fast!

"Next up, Brock with Croagunk," announced Rhonda.

Brock waved, then Croagunk did a hilarious impersonation of a Politoed! He passed with flying colours.

Jessie led Meowth on next, dressed as a Weavile.

"My mega-faceted Meowth can imitate any Pokémon under the sun!"

In seconds, Meowth mimicked a Bulbasaur, a Squirtle and a Togepi!

"Remarkable!" cried the head judge, Mr Sukizo.

Nurse Joy nodded energetically. "I've never seen a Meowth who could imitate other Pokémon until now!"

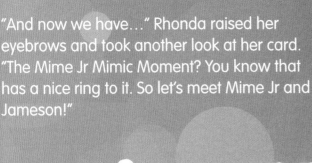

"And now we have…" Rhonda raised her eyebrows and took another look at her card. "The Mime Jr Mimic Moment? You know that has a nice ring to it. So let's meet Mime Jr and Jameson!"

MIME JR

THE PSYCHIC POKÉMON

MIME JR CONFUSES ITS ENEMIES BY MIMICKING THEIR BEHAVIOUR. IT'S MOST EFFECTIVE IN BUSY CROWDS.

Hiding behind a hat and dark glasses, James strutted out from behind the curtain. "If you've got a moment, I've got the mimic!"
James placed Mime Jr on the stage, then reached into his pocket for a floppy grey hat.
"Get ready to witness multiple personalities with just a flick of the wrist!"
Suddenly, Mime Jr spun like a top, transforming itself into Claydol.
The crowd stood up to applaud. James beamed from ear-to-ear – he was a sensation!
Next he turned the hat inside out, revealing a green lining that looked uncannily like a leaf.
James popped it on Mime Jr's head, then turned him round.
"Do Razor Leaf, Chikorita!"
The judges were spellbound. James was going to be a hard act to follow!

PIPLUP
THE PENGUIN POKÉMON

PIPLUP DWELLS ALONG NORTHERN SHORES, DIVING FOR FOOD IN THE CHILLY WATERS. AN ASTONISHINGLY PROUD CREATURE.

Rhonda's eyes twinkled as she introduced the next contestant.

"Next up, it's our winner from last year, the singing Chatot!"

On cue, a small Chatot launched into a splendid rendition of a Jigglypuff song! The defending champion was unanimously voted through. From her spot in the wings, Dawn anxiously adjusted Piplup's costume. A director with a clipboard ushered the duo forward. The spotlights were blinding, but Dawn was determined to give it her best shot.

"A big hand for Piplup dressed up as a Weedle!" beamed Rhonda.

Piplup waddled forward and turned to the side, showing his Weedle bug-suit off to the cameras. The fans cheered – they thought he was cute!

"Thanks!" Dawn clasped her hands in delight. "Piplup, you're a hit!"

Piplup did a victory loop-the-loop, soared to the ceiling then showered the audience with bubbles.

"Oops!" frowned Rhonda. "Weedle can't use Bubblebeam!" The judges cast their votes. Piplup and Dawn were out!

As Dawn and Piplup sadly made their way back to their seats, Ash and Pikachu got ready for their turn.
"Now we're going to see a shape-copying Pikachu!" began Rhonda, looking impressed. "That sounds like a lot of fun!" The crowd clapped warmly as Ash and Pikachu took their places.
"Hey thanks!" laughed Ash. "OK, Seviper!"
Pikachu stretched his chin and his ears back until his face became totally serpentine. Ash punched the air.
"Now Lotad!"
Everyone laughed as Pikachu flattened himself to the floor, then crossed his ears over his head to make Lotad's water lily hat. In seconds, he was Pikachu again and ready for his next pose.

"Wobuffet, Buneary, Mudkip!" directed Ash, as Pikachu changed himself again and again in quick succession.
Ash squinted at the audience. They were going nuts!
"Amazing!" agreed the judges. Ash was through!
Rhonda stepped forward for a close-up shot. "We're going to announce the big winner right after our break!"

93

While the commercials played out, the contestants' dressing room buzzed with excitement. James lifted Mime Jr into the air and twirled him round. "Hurray! We're in it to win it, *big!*"
Jessie glanced at her team-mate and scowled. If she and Meowth were going to win they needed to raise their game! Jessie helped her Pokémon climb into a Sunflora outfit.
"With this look and your voice, it'll be you, me and egg makes three!" she declared confidently.

Meowth smirked. "And Pokémon eggs make a great gift for the Boss!"
"Cut!" spat Jessie. She had no intention of sharing her prize with anyone. "You know we can't give the Boss an unhatched egg!"
Meowth looked confused.
"I do?"
"If we apply some patience we could end up with a legendary Sinnoh superstar Pokémon."

Meowth closed his eyes and imagined a black beast with a mighty tail. "I guess we could take a shot with some of that patience jazz."

"It's now time for the finals!" trilled Rhonda excitedly. "Here are the incredible Pokémon and their trainers who have made it to the last round."
The contestants stood in a line in front of the curtains. Brock winked at Ash. "I'm amazed Croagunk got this far just by pretending to be a Politoed!"
While the defending champion was being invited to perform, Meowth peered over at the prize egg. Its glass case was so close he could almost touch it.
"We don't have to win this silly thing ya know," he hissed at Jessie. "We can grab it then just get outta here fast!"

Jessie looked him in the eye. "Brilliant!"
She suddenly screamed, diverting the crowd so Meowth could knock over the plinth and take a swipe at the egg.

"What are you doing?" demanded James, when his team mates grabbed him by the collar and dragged him towards the exit.

There was utter confusion on stage.
"Croagunk what's wrong?" asked Brock.
The Pokémon beat his froggy hands together, then crawled towards the prize case.
"The egg has GONE!" bellowed Brock. He pointed to the disappearing shapes of Jessie, James and Meowth. "I bet they have got it!"

Officer Jenny leapt out from behind the judge's panel and tossed a Poké Ball after Team Rocket. "They are not going anywhere!"
Her Arcanine immediately pounced forward, stopping the trio in their tracks.
James hugged Mime Jr sulkily, then snarled at Jessie. "If you'd just let us win it, that egg would have been ours peacefully!"

Jessie gritted her teeth. "I'll piece you!"
"Give us back that egg right now!" shouted Ash. He was not going to let his enemies get away with this.
Jessie looked across at Ash with a bored expression. "Time on time it's the same old line. I really would appreciate a little more Twerpish effort."

"Seviper!" commanded Jessie. "Haze, now!"
The massive serpent uncurled, then filled the studio was a suffocating black fog. The audience began to scream in panic.
Ash reached for a Poké Ball of his own. "Staravia, come on out and use Gust!"
Staravia flapped in a loop around the stage, before fanning the fog clear with his powerful wings.

Team Rocket had already disappeared.
"That way!" yelled Ash, pointing towards the exit.
Dawn reached for Piplup, then picked her way out of the audience. "Let's go!"
Rhonda and her crew scrambled after her. "I want every bit of action caught on tape!"

By the time Ash reached the car park, Team Rocket were already floating away in Meowth's hot air balloon.
"Come back here!" he called angrily.
"We gotta leave!" laughed Meowth.
As they sailed away James clutched his Pokémon, still sick at being cheated out of his big moment. "There is but one champ and that champ is you!"

ARCANINE
THE FIRE POKÉMON

ARCANINE IS ONE OF THE FASTEST CREATURES IN THE WORLD AND IT IS SAID CAN TRAVEL UP TO 6,200 MILES IN ONE DAY.

Brock, Ash and Croagunk hurtled after the balloon, while Pikachu and Piplup hitched a ride on Arcanine's back. Dawn and Officer Jenny followed behind.

"Quick Pikachu," instructed Ash. "Use Thunderbolt!" Brock shouted for Ash to hold back. "Using Thunderbolt could damage the egg!"

"You're right!" agreed Ash. He switched to Staravia, sending the Pokémon into a Wing Attack.

Jessie countered with a potent Poison Sting from Dustox. As the moth-like Bug beat Staravia back, she couldn't resist another dig at James.

"Why don't you try doing something with some worth!" she sneered.

James was red-faced. "If you had let Mime Jr emerge victorious we would have!"

"Oh to dream of what might have been!" Jessie teased nastily.

Seeing that Staravia was in trouble, Dawn sent up Piplup. "Quick!" she urged. "Use Bubblebeam on Dustox!" Piplup fired like a pop gun, sending a volley of water bombs into the sky.

Desperate to deflect Piplup, James turned to Mime Jr. "It's time for one of your Mimic Moments!"
The Pokémon blasted the ground with a Bubble Beam move identical to Piplup's! Brock asked Croagunk for help, but all he could do was clap his hands like a Politoed.
"I ley!" cried Brock, bemused. "You can stop now!"
The *Sinnoh Now* crew approached the Team Rocket balloon in their news helicopter. "That Mime Jr has got a super-powerful mimic!" reported Rhonda.
Jessie rolled her eyes. "I've seen better."

"Oh you have?" fumed James. "Well have this. Teeter Dance!" Suddenly Mime Jr began to dance, casting a strange spell over the other Pokémon riding in the balloon. Meowth and Dustox were compelled to dance from side to side against their will. As Meowth's paws were torn away from the controls, the balloon tumbled into freefall.
Jessie was boiling with rage. "Those Twerps are so far away they don't feel a thing!"

Ash and his friends stared up at the sinking balloon.

"It looks like it's going to crash!" boomed Brock.

"If that happens the Pokémon egg is done for," warned Dawn.

"Noooooo!" came a cry from the distance.

As the balloon lurched to one side, Jessie had let the egg fall through her hands.

Dawn acted fast. "Quick Buneary, Bounce!" Buneary bounded into the air, safely catching the egg in her soft paws.

The friends cheered. "All right!"

Rhonda's helicopter circled the group.

"Their quick-thinking saved the Pokémon egg!"

"Great catch!" grinned Ash. "Now we're all clear Pikachu, use Thunderbolt!"

Pikachu focussed, then blasted the balloon with a supercharged surge of electricity.

"Leaving the egg without knowing what it will hatch into stinks!" shouted Jessie, as Team Rocket disappeared over the horizon.

BUNEARY
A RABBIT POKÉMON

BUNEARY ROLLS UP ITS EARS THEN SHARPLY RELEASES THEM TO LASH OUT. ITS SPECIAL MOVE IS THE DIZZY PUNCH.

James looked down at Meowth and the shredded balloon. "I wish we could say the same about you!"

Back at the studio, it was finally time to discover who the winner would be.

"It's been a remarkable Dress-up Contest," confirmed Rhonda. "But the votes are now in!"

Dawn was too nervous to look. "Pikachu was great, but I bet that Chatot has won again."

The spotlights flickered between the contestants in an agonising wait. At last, Officer Jenny announced, "And this year's big winner is Brock's Croagunk!"

"No way?" burst out Brock. Nurse Joy smiled and nodded. "Croagunk stayed in character during the entire contest. Well done!"

Piplup and Dawn hugged. "Isn't this great!"

"Brock, way ta go!" laughed Ash.

While Croagunk faced the audience and clapped his hands in Politoed style, Mr Sukizo presented Brock with the egg. "A brand new Pokémon Dress-up legend is born!" declared Rhonda. "We hope you've enjoyed the Contest coverage for this year!"

Brock's surprise at receiving first prize has left our heroes with another tantalising question – what kind of Pokémon will the Dress-up Contest egg produce?

EVOLUTIONS WORDSEARCH

Use the Sinnoh Pokédex and your skills as a Trainer to work out which Pokémon are hiding in this wordsearch. Fill the right evolutions into each set then mark the names off on the letter grid. The names could be hiding vertically, horizontally, diagonally or even back-to-front!

```
P Z S W O N S A M O B A
J U V B P N Z J A H I P
T I L Y D Y I R C R D S
O D Q P I O S X H A O N
R B X W N X U W O H O E
T U R T W I G G P C F U
E U M F T L R K A M I Q
R F G S K J C P V I H I
R O S E L I A E D H S P
A S Q H E R J K F C X S
B W K L B Q N O T V R E
K R I C K E T U N E H V
```

SNOVER – _ _ _ _ _ _ _ _ _

_ _ _ _ _ _ _ _ – MACHOKE – MACHAMP

KRICKETOT – _ _ _ _ _ _ _ _ _ _ _

BUDEW – _ _ _ _ _ _ _ **– ROSERADE**

_ _ _ _ _ _ _ _ _ **– GROTLE –** _ _ _ _ _ _ _ _ _

_ _ _ _ _ _ _ **– BIBAREL**

PIPLUP – _ _ _ _ _ _ _ _ _ **– EMPOLEON**

COMBEE – _ _ _ _ _ _ _ _ _ _

_ _ _ _ _ **– STEELIX**

_ _ _ _ _ _ _ _ _ **– MONFERNO – INFERNAPE**

121 GIRAFARIG

TYPE:	NORMAL-PSYCHIC
ABILITY:	INNER FOCUS-EARLY BIRD
HEIGHT:	1.5m
WEIGHT:	41.5kg

Girafarig's seeing tail also contains a small, but alert brain. The Pokémon uses its unique extra head to bite any would-be attackers that try and creep up on it.

122 HIPPOPOTAS

TYPE:	GROUND
ABILITY:	SAND STREAM
HEIGHT:	0.8m
WEIGHT:	49.5kg

This Pokémon is only sighted in dry places. It covers itself in sand to protect itself from germs. When it gets hot, Hippopotas expels grains of dust instead of sweat.

123 HIPPOWDON

TYPE:	GROUND
ABILITY:	SAND STREAM
HEIGHT:	2m
WEIGHT:	300kg

Hippowdon's vast jaws have enough power to totally crush a car. It has the ability to blast its foes with awesome sand twisters. Hippowdon is evolved from Hippopotas.

124 AZURILL

TYPE:	NORMAL
ABILITY:	THICK FAT-HUGE POWER
HEIGHT:	0.2m
WEIGHT:	2kg

Azurill prefers to dwell near water. It moves around on land by bouncing up and down on its bulbous tail. The Pokémon evolves into a Marill and then an Azumarill.

125 MARILL

TYPE:	WATER
ABILITY:	THICK FAT-HUGE POWER
HEIGHT:	0.4m
WEIGHT:	8.5kg

Marill is most agile when swimming. Its tail makes a useful float when it dives underwater. Marill forages for plants that grow at the bottom of river beds.

126 AZUMARILL

TYPE:	WATER
ABILITY:	THICK FAT-HUGE POWER
HEIGHT:	0.8m
WEIGHT:	28.5kg

This Pokémon frequents rivers, lakes and ponds. Azumarill is very difficult to spot in the water – its blue colouring and patterns have camouflaged it from many enemies.

127 SKORUPI

TYPE:	POISON-BUG
ABILITY:	BATTLE ARMOUR-SNIPER
HEIGHT:	0.8m
WEIGHT:	12kg

Skorupi fools its victims by burying itself in sand and lying in wait until the perfect moment arises. It then grips its prey with its tail claws and injects them with poison.

128 DRAPION

TYPE:	POISON-DARK
ABILITY:	BATTLE ARMOUR-SNIPER
HEIGHT:	1.3m
WEIGHT:	61.5kg

Girafarig's seeing tail also contains a small, but alert brain. The Pokémon uses its unique extra head to bite any would-be attackers that try and creep up on it.

129 CROAGUNK

TYPE:	POISON-FIGHTING
ABILITY:	ANTICIPATION-DRY SKIN
HEIGHT:	0.7m
WEIGHT:	23kg

Croagunk has poison sacs within its cheeks. These sacs can be inflated, causing the Pokémon to emit an unnerving, blubbery sound. It also jabs with its toxic fingers.

130 TOXICROAK

TYPE:	POISON-FIGHTING
ABILITY:	ANTICIPATION-DRY SKIN
HEIGHT:	1.3m
WEIGHT:	44.4kg

The poison in Toxicroak's sacs is pumped to its knuckle claws via tubes inside its arms. Just one scratch from these claws can prove fatal. It is evolved from Croagunk.

131 CARNIVINE

TYPE:	GRASS
ABILITY:	LEVITATE
HEIGHT:	1.4m
WEIGHT:	27kg

As it uses its tentacles to hang from tree branches, Carnivine looks like a plant. It attracts passing prey with its sweet-smelling saliva, before swallowing them whole.

132 REMORAID

TYPE:	WATER
ABILITY:	HUSTLE-SNIPER
HEIGHT:	0.6m
WEIGHT:	12kg

Remoraid has a well-developed mouth that it relies on during combat. It can squirt water from it with such force, any flying prey are instantly shot down.

133 OCTILLERY

TYPE:	WATER
ABILITY:	SUCTION CUPS-SNIPER
HEIGHT:	0.9m
WEIGHT:	28.5kg

Octillery lurks in the gaps between boulders or in holes dotted along the sea floor. It uses its powerful suction cups to grip prey. It is evolved from Remoraid.

134 FINNEON

TYPE:	WATER
ABILITY:	SWIFT SWIM-STORM DRAIN
HEIGHT:	0.4m
WEIGHT:	7kg

Nicknamed 'Beautifly of the sea', Finneon possesses a patterned double tail fin that shines vividly after dark. The Pokémon evolves into a Lumineon.

135 LUMINEON

TYPE:	WATER
ABILITY:	SWIFT SWIM-STORM DRAIN
HEIGHT:	1.2m
WEIGHT:	24kg

When it needs to hide, Lumineon crawls along the deep sea floor using the two small fins on its chest. It attracts prey by flashing patterns on its four striking tail fins.

136 TENTACOOL

TYPE:	WATER-POISON
ABILITY:	CLEAR BODY-LIQUID OOZE
HEIGHT:	0.9m
WEIGHT:	45.5kg

Tentacool's body is composed of nearly 100% water. It has the power to shoot strange beams of light from its crystal-like eyes. It evolves into a Tentacruel.

137 TENTACRUEL

TYPE:	WATER-POISON
ABILITY:	CLEAR BODY-LIQUID OOZE
HEIGHT:	1.6m
WEIGHT:	55kg

This vicious Pokémon uses its 80 tentacles to ensnare its victims. No prey can escape until they are utterly weakened by Tentacruel's natural poison.

138 FEEBAS

TYPE:	WATER
ABILITY:	SWIFT SWIM
HEIGHT:	0.6m
WEIGHT:	7.4kg

Feebas is famous for its shabby colours and dishevelled appearance. It tends to gather in shoals in fixed regions and locations. It evolves into a Milotic.

139 MILOTIC

TYPE:	WATER
ABILITY:	MARVEL SCALE
HEIGHT:	6.2m
WEIGHT:	162kg

When humans argue and bicker, it is said that Milotic will rise from the depths of lakes to becalm their violent hearts. Its stunning blue and red tail is legendary.

140 MANTYKE

TYPE:	WATER-FLYING
ABILITY:	SWIFT SWIM-WATER ABSORB
HEIGHT:	1m
WEIGHT:	65kg

Mantyke is a friendly Pokémon that uses its antennae to capture the subtle flows of seawater. The patterns on its back vary by region. It evolves into a Mantine.

141 MANTINE

TYPE:	WATER-FLYING
ABILITY:	SWIFT SWIM-WATER ABSORB
HEIGHT:	2.1m
WEIGHT:	220kg

Mantine are vast seabeasts, but they have an unusual grace in the water. If the sea is calm there is a chance of encountering a swarm swimming as if they are in flight.

142 SNOVER

TYPE:	GRASS-ICE
ABILITY:	SNOW WARNING
HEIGHT:	1m
WEIGHT:	50.5kg

Although it generally lives alone on snowy mountains, Snover is boldly curious if it comes into contact with humans. This Pokémon evolves into an Abomasnow.

143 ABOMASNOW

TYPE:	GRASS-ICE
ABILITY:	SNOW WARNING
HEIGHT:	2.2m
WEIGHT:	135.5kg

This is the legendary abominable snowman. Abomasnow whips up mountain blizzards, blanketing vast areas in snow. It is also called the 'Ice Monster'.

144 SNEASEL

TYPE:	DARK-ICE
ABILITY:	INNER FOCUS-KEEN EYE
HEIGHT:	0.9m
WEIGHT:	28kg

Sneasel is a thief, feeding on eggs stolen from other Pokémon nests. It uses its sharply-hooked claws to swipe at its adversaries. It evolves into a Weavile.

145 WEAVILE

TYPE:	DARK-ICE
ABILITY:	PRESSURE
HEIGHT:	1.1m
WEIGHT:	34kg

Weaville hunts in cold climes, operating in efficient packs of four or five. It has learnt to carve messages to its pack-mates by scraping patterns on frost-covered trees.

146 UXIE

TYPE:	PSYCHIC
ABILITY:	LEVITATE
HEIGHT:	0.3m
WEIGHT:	0.3kg

There is a common belief that Uxie can wipe out the memory of those who see its eyes. It is said to be the 'Being of Knowledge', helping humans improve their lives.

147 MESPRIT

TYPE:	PSYCHIC
ABILITY:	LEVITATE
HEIGHT:	0.3m
WEIGHT:	0.3kg

Mesprit sleeps at the bottom of a lake. It is often spoken of as the 'Being of Emotion', credited with teaching people the true nobility of sorrow, pain and joy.

148 AZELF

TYPE:	PSYCHIC
ABILITY:	LEVITATE
HEIGHT:	0.3m
WEIGHT:	0.3kg

Azelf is the 'Being of Willpower'. It sleeps so that it can keep the world in balance. It is widely believed that Uxie, Mesprit and Azelf all came from the same egg.

149 DIALGA

TYPE:	STEEL-DRAGON
ABILITY:	PRESSURE
HEIGHT:	5.4m
WEIGHT:	683kg

This mythical Pokémon is spoken of in legend and is thought to posses the power to control time itself.

150 PALKIA

TYPE:	WATER-DRAGON
ABILITY:	PRESSURE
HEIGHT:	4.2m
WEIGHT:	336kg

The mythical Pokémon lives in a gap in the spatial dimension that runs parallel to our own. Palkia has the ability to distort space.

151 MANAPHY

TYPE:	WATER
ABILITY:	HYDRATION
HEIGHT:	0.3m
WEIGHT:	1.4kg

Manaphy will swim vast distances to return to its birthplace. Being water-based, Manaphy is easily affected by its environment.

WHO IS DARKRAI?

DARKRAI...

TYPE:	DARK
ABILITY:	PITCH-BLACK
HEIGHT:	1.5m
WEIGHT:	50.5kg

Is this creature friend or foe? Folklore has it that on moonless nights, this Pokémon has the power to bewitch people with strange nightmares. Look out for Darkrai, it is a force that cannot be ignored...

LETTER LINK MYSTERY

A new Pokémon is soon to reveal itself, but what is its name? To discover its identity fill your answers into this grid, then read down the highlighted letters.

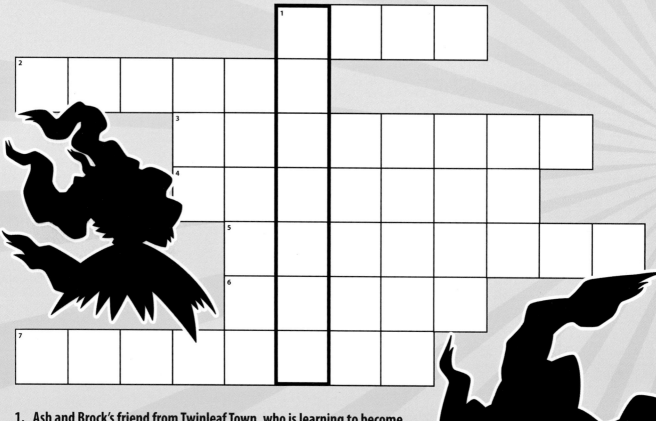

1. Ash and Brock's friend from Twinleaf Town, who is learning to become a Pokémon Co-ordinator.
2. The presenter of TV show 'Sinnoh Now'.
3. Someone who cares for the sick and injured.
4. Ash's favourite Pokémon.
5. The Sinnoh city that has a Rock-type gym.
6. Jessie and Meowth's partner-in-crime.
7. Officer Jenny's proud Fire Pokémon.

ANSWERS

Page 12: Pokédex challenge
Answers: 1-D, 2-E, 3-A, 4-B, 5-C

Page 18: Crazy colour

Page 19: Stop Team Rocket!
Answers: SLY, DEVIOUS, CHEATING,
LAZY, SCHEMING, JEALOUS, DISLOYAL,
MEAN, SELFISH, THOUGHTLESS, HARSH,
DISHONEST.

Pages 36-37: Rock-hard anagrams
Answers: GRAVELER, BONSLY, BASTIODON,
CRANIDOS, SHIELDON, SUDOWOODO,
RAMPARDOS, GEODUDE, ONIX, GOLEM.
Roark played GEODUDE, ONIX, and
CRANIDOS.

Page 42: Dawn's dash

Page 43: Mime Jr Spot the difference

Page 60: Pokémon time challenge.
Answer: Dozens of words can be made from
this phrase. Here's 12 to get you started:
1-Sack, 2-Whip, 3-Tailback, 4-Capable,
5-Cash, 6-Tablet, 7-Patch, 8-Sale, 9-Wits,
10-Hatch, 11-Alphabet, 12-Backlash...

Page 61: Battle moves

Page 84: Double Team Aipom
Answer: 13 Times as one is the real Aipom

Page 85: Crosswords with Brock

Page 102-103: Evolutions wordsearch

Page 107: Letter link mystery